**Other books by the author:**

*New Testament Exposition: From Text to Sermon*

*Daughters of the Church: Women and Ministry From New Testament Times to the Present (with Ruth Tucker)*

*Interpreting the Book of Acts*

*Ephesians*

*1 & 2 Timothy/Titus:* The NIV Application Commentary

*Luke: The Expositor's Bible Commentary* (with David W. Pao)

"A Plural Ministry View" in *Women in Ministry: Four Views*, edited by Bonnidell Clouse and Robert G. Clouse.

# DIRECTION

A Biblical Perspective on Being Called and Sent by God

# WALTER L. LIEFELD

WESTBOW&#42;
PRESS
A DIVISION OF THOMAS NELSON
& ZONDERVAN

WestBow Press books may be ordered through
booksellers or by contacting:

WestBow Press
A Division of Thomas Nelson & Zondervan
1663 Liberty Drive
Bloomington, IN 47403
www.westbowpress.com
1 (866) 928-1240

ISBN: 978-1-4908-6207-1 (sc)
ISBN: 978-1-4908-6206-4 (e)

Library of Congress Control Number: 2014921560

Printed in the United States of America.

WestBow Press rev. date: 02/09/2015

# Contents

# Acknowledgments

Olive Fleming Liefeld, my wife, has been outstanding as my encourager and editor.

My grateful thanks go to Dr. Linda Cannell for her comprehensive editing from her own wide experience. Beverly Hancock, my daughter; her husband, Jonathan for their help with computer editing and suggestions. My son, David Liefeld, and his wife, Robin, for their ideas in the initial draft and help with the title. Mark Veeneman, for being my encourager and constant friend.

I am especially grateful to Dr. Thomas Keppeler, who took time out of his busy ministry at Elmbrook Church to write chapter 6, "Case Study: A Sending Church." His firsthand experience and advanced thinking have been invaluable.

# Introduction

Peter Fleming intended to be a professor. His studies at the University of Washington were preparing him well for this goal. How far would he go? He had already pursued American literature and philosophy and had secured a master's degree in English literature. Now he was considering the next step, and he believed God was leading him to seminary. His girlfriend, Olive Ainslie, was waiting for his decision. But something—or someone—intervened.

Pete was learning about the unreached savage Auca people in Ecuador from his long-time friend, Jim Elliot. Jim talked about going as a single man to reach these people and was looking for another single man to go with him. When Pete heard this, he believed God was calling him to fill that role. Pete's church leaders did not encourage him to go with Jim at first, as they saw him as a teacher in the university world. But now that calling had became less sure for Pete. Finally, his elders commended him to the work in Ecuador. His commitment to Olive was rather abruptly dismissed. From then on, all attention was on Ecuador.

By the time the Aucas were found, the missionaries who answered the call to reach them had grown from just Jim and Pete to Ed McCully, Nate Saint, and Roger Youderian. On January 8, 1956, these five men were killed by the Aucas. Was Pete mistaken about his earlier sense of calling to reach the Aucas? And did the great movement in missions that resulted from the five killings require their deaths?

On Olive's part, after two and a half years of preparation waiting to go to Ecuador, she had finally joined Pete. But after her arrival in Ecuador, she experienced so much sickness due to the altitude that she began to question whether God had really called her there. Had she gone only because of Pete? Now she was holding him back from his ministry among the jungle people. It was not until over a year later, when Pete and the other four men were on the river beach in Auca territory, that she was reading in 2 Corinthians 5 and God's call was confirmed for her. She read, "He who prepared us for this very thing is God" (RSV). She had the assurance that God had called *her,* even though, days later, the bodies of Pete and the others were found in the river near the beach.

What assurance did Olive have now regarding her call to Ecuador? Had that call changed, or had this been the preparation for something further? A few months later, she returned home and was surprised to find that people knew about the five men being killed because of all the newspaper and TV coverage. She was met by TV reporters at the airport for an interview. That was the beginning of many interviews and speaking engagements, both secular and in church groups. It was not what she had expected, and she was not immediately prepared for it. People were interested in this story but could not understand why those men would go out to such savage Indians. This opened up a new world and a new opportunity for her to share the message of God's love. She believed that God now had called her to tell this story.

I knew of Olive through the story of the five men but never heard her speak. I had prayed to meet her, but it seemed very unlikely. When we finally did meet, it was not planned by either of us. However, both of us believed that God had arranged our meeting, and we were married a few months later. Was Olive Fleming's marriage to me foreseen and planned by God? Were our three children—David, Beverly, and Holly—and our seven grandchildren also in those plans?

For over fifty years, Olive and I have lived with these questions. And for most of those years, I have been thinking of writing a book. But this book is not the same as I had intended. As I proceeded with calling, I became more interested with sending. I have chosen not to deal with some issues related to calling, including some that others have already explored. Eventually, I invited my friend Tom Keppeler to offer some thoughts on that topic. I trust you will be excited by the results.

For many years, writers have struggled with the ideas of calling and sending, without bringing the two together. Of these, sending has received the most attention. That is natural. The more emphasis that has been given to missions, the more that has been heard about sending. Few writers have dealt with calling, except for a rather thin treatment here and there, somewhat like an evangelistic invitation following a weak sermon. The time has come for a thorough treatment of calling throughout Scripture. At the same time, rather than a mere repetition of information about sending, that topic receives a reworking that applies it to the contemporary scene.

My earliest clear church memory was of attending a service in a Baptist church in New York City when I was about four years old. I can recall specifically where I was sitting. Although I did not go to church often, I was taught the Bible at home. At the age of ten, I asked God to save me—the result of a footnote! I was reading a simple book with many footnotes. I looked up one that took me to John 3:7. It told me that I "must be born again." That marked my salvation, and a few years later, I was regularly attending a community Bible church.

During the intervening years, I took in the messages in the church and grew spiritually. When we moved to another church, I was eager to move ahead. While in high school, I was baptized. Life at school was exciting, but I never lost that faith. I went on to college at New York University, Shelton College, and Columbia University. I learned that I had several abilities, including music. I studied voice, organ, and conducting and led two choirs. Eventually, I was ordained, and over the years, I preached everywhere, from the street corner near my home to pulpits of every major denomination. My first church was Northport Baptist Church on Long Island, and my first teaching position was at Shelton College.

This was also a time of further study. Greek and Latin and related courses at Columbia University and Union Theological Seminary, eventually led me to a PhD.

During this time, I met Olive Fleming and was certain God had led us together. We were married in 1959, ready to serve the Lord together. Our first two children, David and Beverly, were born in Long Island, New York, while I was pastor of a church in Sea Cliff. Our third child, Holly, was born later, in the Chicago area, where I had begun teaching Greek and New Testament at Trinity Evangelical Divinity School in 1963. During all this time, I had little sense of being called but a deep sense of God's place in my life. On reflection, I think that the prayers of two godly parents affected me at every point.

Our experiences during our time at Trinity, where I taught for thirty-one years, included planting a church in Arlington Heights, Illinois, spending a year in Germany on sabbatical, and preaching and teaching on five continents. These activities, along with serving five years as pastor at Christ Church Lake Forest, all helped me grow in Christ. This is not intended just to list experiences but to say that every move, every experience, and every conversation gave opportunity to hear and respond to the call of God. That means that in my long life (eighty-seven years now) there were few major moves and few major events but rather a series of experiences of God's grace. Many of these were great opportunities for spiritual growth. After our retirement, we have spent almost equal time successively in three lively churches. I can honestly say that all of them have contributed to our spiritual growth. God is good indeed. We recently moved to a new location, ready to start a new phase of life.

So was Peter Fleming called? Am I called? Or was my wife, Olive, called? Pete believed it was God's call for him to go to the Aucas, where he was killed at age twenty-seven, and both Olive and I have watched God unfold each step of our call together for fifty-five years.

This book is written to allow you to experience my lifetime of study and teaching of God's Word. You will notice that I am using some personal pronouns, such as *you* and *I*. This is perhaps unusual in a book that deals with issues and topics. I do it deliberately so that we can explore all this together.

Do I need the same kind of calling, whether I am considering studying Greek or theology or applying for a research position in Germany? What sort of call would lead to working with the InterVarsity Christian Fellowship among graduate students? The questions could continue. Does missionary work in Thailand require the same kind of calling as pastoral ministry in Northport, or does neither of these require any special calling? Is there a different set of questions and answers for Koreans than for Canadians? Does one need a call from God to be a lifetime missionary overseas but not for a short-term mission building houses in Mexico? Does a pastor need a call but an elder or a Sunday school teacher does not?

Our exploration of Scripture, theology, and some personal experiences should help us develop answers clear enough to address these sorts of questions and to take the next steps in our own journey. This book provides an orientation to the subject and I hope that in the discussions that follow we shall be able to progress together toward definitions and a means of discernment of God's call.

# 1

# The Meaning of Calling

The assumption that a call, as traditionally defined, exists and is absolutely essential for ministry, plunges one into a whirlpool of conflicting opinions.

The concept of being called is not unique to Christians. Ask people in North America about their calling, and they will tell you about their vocations and how they chose them, and they will describe their interesting characteristics. Even a man known in his African community as a fetish priest, a role close to what we know as a witch doctor, articulated his call. In a translated conversation, he told me how he came into that position. One day when he had gone down to the river, he drowned and had stayed drowned for three days. Then he came to life again. The village leaders, upon hearing his experience, invited him to be their fetish priest. With significant differences, this sounds, of course, like the death and resurrection of Christ.

Some months after my return from Africa, it struck me that he had described what in our religious vocabulary would be designated a call. I had been interviewing people for several years about their calls to Christian ministry. Now, without expecting it, I had heard what, in effect, was the alleged call of a man in a totally different religious context to a position of supreme religious influence in his community. According to his story, his acceptance into a present position of immense authority depended on an alleged supernatural experience.

Ask Christian missionaries, pastors, or youth workers about their callings, and the responses will be on how God brought them into their present ministries. This book is about them, and much more.

In the New Testament, the word *called* does not identify any special class of believers. What it does do is focus, from time to time, on believers who have specially earned that designation or who, by their lives or actions, have demonstrated its benefits. Perhaps its value can be seen by comparing it to the experience of being loved but not married. The latter accurately identifies one who legally is so designated; one either is or is not married. But one can be loved (called) whether married or not. All Christians are called (loved) though their enjoyment of being called by God can vary greatly. I hope that the beneficial effect of calling will increase mightily through the reading of this book.


# Decision Making

Decisions, decisions! Religious choices, friends, major purchases, living standards and locations, education, life partner—these and thousands of other big and small options face us over a lifetime. For the earnest Christian, decisions involve prayerful dependence on God and for most of us, some more visible sign of God's will and direction would be welcome!

The sermons, articles, and books on the subject of discerning the will of God are endless, yet their very existence demonstrates the need. The literature reflects two polar opposite views: First, God has a specific will at every turn, and we must daily seek to be in the center of God's will. And second, there is really no such center, but there may be several alternatives. Using our God-given wisdom, we prayerfully and carefully choose (perhaps daily) the alternative we believe will most honor God. In-between these are mediating views that combine, in some measure, common sense with specific guidance from God.

The one decision I have been asked for counsel about most in my successive ministries as an InterVarsity staff member, seminary professor, and pastor has to do with what is best described as calling. This relates to our life vocation (or vocations) and sets the stage for all other decisions. Determining our calling is a comprehensive and life-changing decision. It involves both discovery and response. That process can be a gradual unfolding or an instant event. It can be unremarkable, or it can be dramatic. In contrast to choosing a vocation, most decisions have only a limited effect on our lives. Of course, a decision to drive while drunk can cause an accident that is life changing and perhaps life ending. Some decisions that are made with little forethought can have far-reaching effects. Other decisions can often be modified, changed, or reversed. By its very nature (and to explore that nature is one purpose of this book), calling is not something one can reverse because it is from God.

I might as well tell you up front that this opening section is hard to write because it has to presume, dodge, or explain certain aspects and views of calling before having the opportunity to explore them. I do not want to lead you, my reader, into some simple one-two-three method of discerning God's call. We need to build on a foundation of Scripture and theology. Nor do I want us to get lost in a maze of doctrinal corridors that leave us confused when we ask the practical questions. Certainly, it seems that it would be a lot easier for us if we all had some extraordinary experience—a vision or a voice, a burning bush perhaps—to make it unmistakably clear. But don't we walk by faith in the matter of calling as well as in other aspects of life?

You have noticed that the word *calling* in my chapter title is in quotation marks. That in itself reflects one of the issues we will address in future chapters. Is there a distinctive call that separates all Christians into one of two groups: those called to ministry or missions and those who may live deeply spiritual yet ordinary lives? This raises other questions. Is the outward distinguishing feature between these two groups ordination? If I believe God wants me to serve with a para-church group rather than with a church or denomination, should I still be ordained? I will address this and other questions in the following chapters.

**What Issues Do I Face?**

"So you are going to study geology!" The speaker was one of my high school teachers. I had met him when I returned a year or so after my graduation. He asked what my future goals were, and I had rather clumsily said, "Theology." By the time he had gone on to congratulate me on entering such an interesting field as geology (and a lucrative one if I were to get a job with an oil company), I did not have the inclination to trigger another long discourse by telling him that he had misunderstood.

But could I have entered the field of geology instead of theology and still considered it a calling from God? (In fact, I did take some courses in geology at the university, and faculty members there tried to persuade me to major in that science.) Recent writers and others, such as Martin Luther, have assured us correctly that God's calling extends to all Christians and that we can serve God wherever we are. Given that fact, however, is there still some special call of God to Christian ministry?

Some years later, after I had served as an InterVarsity staff member and then as a pastor, I decided to accept an invitation to teach at Trinity Evangelical Divinity School. I excitedly told friends of my decision, only to be informed by the mother of one of them how disappointed she was that I was leaving the ministry. This narrows things even further. Is ministry only the pastorate or perhaps overseas missions? No, once again many voices are assuring us today that ministry is a broad category and that all Christians have some ministry, just as all have received some spiritual gift.

And so we ask, "Does God extend a special call to some to do pastoral work or missions or maybe seminary teaching, a calling that is different from a call to teach Sunday school or to do a three-week mission some summer?" Is calling a matter of using one's God-given judgment or of sensing some special leading of the Spirit? Is a call to ministry or missions a lifetime calling? Can one instead be called to missions on a short-term basis? Is it unspiritual to serve for a time in missions (or some other ministry) and then pursue some secular vocation? Do Christians need a special call to missions, or does the Great Commission in itself constitute that call, with only the designation of method and geography remaining to be learned? Should the church have a role in confirming a call to ministry in a para-church organization?

If, as the Bible teaches, every Christian believer is called by God and can serve God in secular as well as religious occupations, is there still a special call to ministry and global mission? If the answer to that is yes, and if I think I am called in this way, how can I have certain assurance of my calling? An inner voice, a sign from heaven, some unusual circumstance, a heart concern for a particular ministry or people, being significantly gifted—is one or more of these the way to know I am called? Conversely, how can the church know whom among its members God has called? What are the means of discerning a person's genuine call? And if God has called, how can the church *send*?

If there is no special calling, what means are left for a Christian to choose correctly between alternative paths for serving God? How does one decide, for example, whether to continue witnessing in some store or business here or to pack up and fly halfway around the world to evangelize an unreached tribe? On the church's part, what are the criteria for determining if some church member seeks guidance but lacks a special divine calling? How does the church decide whether to commit funds and to offer wholehearted practical and spiritual support to that individual?

Such dilemmas are not going to be solved by neat formulas, by anecdotal experiences of spiritual giants, or even by recourse to this or that favorite biblical text. For earnest Christians seeking to determine whether they have a call, and for churches that anguish over a request for support by someone who feels called but seems unqualified, the whole matter of calling can be a frustrating mystery.

If we think that God does call some people in a special way to various ministries, certain issues remain that are not easily resolved. What ministries require such a call? Is an internal sense of calling sufficient? How does one discern an internal or secret calling? Is that too subjective to rely on? Should one seek objective indications, such as signs? Is ecclesiastical concurrence necessary? To what extent do abilities, spiritual gifts, and circumstances indicate a viable career option for a person who is willing?

Why is the nature of the call a mystery to so many people? Why is it that even seminary students, whom we might expect to be fairly certain in this regard, are so often perplexed as to their calling? Why do some candidates for ordination, who ideally are mature, spiritual individuals, fumble when asked by an ordination council to tell about their call to ministry? *Calling needs to be demystified.* Actually, it was my extensive experiences in talking with my seminary students that convinced me that more discussion and clarification of issues surrounding calling is needed. The ever-present, fallible human factor adds to the confusion. Some earnest Christians are so eager to serve the Lord that they confuse that desire with the call of God. Others who do not feel called are told by their pastors or others that they are so gifted they should choose a ministerial vocation. Missionary conferences can present world needs so vividly that participants are almost ashamed not to consider themselves called.

It is generally assumed that in order to serve in church ministry, a person needs "the call to the ministry." Today's generation takes it pretty much for granted that options in church ministries are multifaceted, so *the* ministry tends to give way to ministries (or simply ministry) without the definite article. The same is *not* the case with calling. Whether regarding church ministry or global ministries, we still speak of *the* call. Part of the mystery in calling is trying to discern whether it is concerns, passions, and an eagerness to serve that may be driving us, not the call. We search the Scriptures to find examples of a call to see if we fit the mold. This puts us in danger of what is sometimes called attribution. That is, when we read of a life-changing encounter between a person (whether in Bible history or contemporary) and God, we are likely to attribute that encounter to *the* call (e.g., to foreign missions). Conversely, and specifically in biblical narratives, we want to attribute what we conceive to be the characteristics of the call to such encounters, even if calling terminology is not present. Put another way, we are too ready to identify divine-human conversations as a call.

We are not nitpicking about petty points of semantics. It should be clear that calling terminology requires serious study and that its meaning, whether we realize it or not, is ambiguous. We sometimes use it generally and sometimes specifically (e.g., calling and the call). Calling needs to be analyzed, with perhaps the substitution of one or more other terms, at least in discussion, to distinguish its various aspects. This of course is not a denial that God calls. Quite the opposite. God does call, and in fact, the whole Christian life is a calling from God. But it is common to isolate (and standardize) a call to particular service, separating it from God's immense, comprehensive calling to us all. Worse, some have elevated the call to the ministry *above* the calling of those in the workplace. The way a church conceives of ordination relates to that perspective.

Conversely, we can so generalize God's calling that we fail to account for the fact that, biblically, there are those to whom God has assigned special ministries that others do not have. We can also ignore that in the Bible the *sending* of people into various kinds of service to God is mentioned more frequently than is calling, and this sending is of immense importance. Of course, sending requires a sender and, biblically the church should be proactive in that process—a fact that we will explore extensively later on.

Theologians have written about an internal call, but since we are human and sinful, the subjectivity of an internal call (was that God's voice or my imagination?) can result in uneasy perplexity. The sad instances of earnest Christians who have given up almost everything to follow what they thought was a call, only to end in failure, suggests that something is lacking in our common understanding of calling. The result can be wasted lives and wasted resources.

A call to ministry, however one may define it, is only one aspect of God's multifaceted call to all his people. It is essential that those who seek an understanding of their personal, vocational calling refrain from rushing into a self-centered quest that bypasses a realization of God's magnificent, sovereign role as the God who calls. He does this in various ways. God calls through natural revelation, "what has been made." He calls all his creatures to acknowledge his "invisible qualities—his eternal power and divine nature" (Rom. 1:20). He calls sinners to salvation. The Lord Jesus said that no one comes to him whom the Father has not given him (John 6:44). Romans 8:39, 9:12, 24, 25, 26, and 11:29 and Galatians 5:8 are significant here. God calls us to eternal life, to hope, and to glory (Eph. 1:18; 2 Thess. 2:14; 1 Tim. 6:12; 1 Pet. 5:10). He also calls us to a life of holiness, to Christian character. Note Romans 1:7, which says, "To all in Rome who are loved by God and called to be his holy people." First Corinthians 1:2 is addressed "to the church of God in Corinth, to those sanctified in Christ Jesus and called to be his holy people." Our primary call relates to character, what we are, not to service, what we do. "He has saved us and called us to a holy life" (2 Tim. 1:9). We have been set apart for this life of holiness (sanctified). The fact that this same theme and the combination of calling with a reference to holiness also occurs in different contexts in 1 Thessalonians 4:7 and in 1 Peter 1:15 demonstrates its importance. We are also called to follow Jesus as our example for doing good, even while suffering (1 Peter 2:21). It is premature, incongruous, and delusional to expect a call to ministry until we have heeded the call to personal holiness.

Should we then be thinking about calling just in terms of full-time service, specifically to pastoral ministry, or even more narrowly to ministry in a particular church? In most Protestant groups, churches call pastors. (In others, a bishop or equivalent church official designates the pastor.) And they usually are seeking a pastor who will stay for a period of at least five years or so. Should a candidate for a pastoral position then have a clear sense of call to that church as well as to pastoral ministry in general? And should they have their own sense as to the probable length of service there, or should they accept the church's parameters as defining the call?

A man was interviewed by the search committee of a church for the position of senior pastor. There was no question in his mind that he had been called to ministry as such, and he felt called to that church. However, he also believed he should encourage the committee to articulate their sense as to whether God had called him there. He was actually looking beyond the initial decision regarding the choice of pastor and was trying to stimulate a collegial atmosphere in discussing the goals he and the church might pursue together. Apparently, some on that committee were disconcerted by his insistence that they too should have a sense of calling and that the church and pastor should work out vision, goals, and plans together. They therefore lost him with all he could do, and he lost a great opportunity for service.

**Primary Question:** If there is such a call, how does God go about issuing it? Although we do not want to probe inappropriately into God's mind to determine how he chooses to work, we can study God's own revelation in the Bible. We can scan the Scriptures for instances of God's calling activity and thereby not only know something of that activity but know God better. Moses prayed, "If you are pleased with me, teach me your ways so that I may know you and continue to find favor with you" (Ex. 33:13). It is as we observe and are taught God's ways that we understand him better. Of course, we must not assume that God always works in the same way. One of the areas in the study of the book of Acts where discernment is needed is in distinguishing between what is prescriptive, intended to give us direction to follow exactly, and what is descriptive, which, while teaching us, does not present a model to be copied exactly. But even where we do not expect God to act in an identical manner, we can learn about him by observing his acts in history, especially his acts among his people.

Even though God can be observed to call people who are not outstanding, or whose lives are not perfect, two things are clear. First, as 1 Corinthians 1 points out, the power in their lives is his, not theirs. Second, his choices are validated by the devotion of those chosen. The glory always must ultimately go to God; otherwise, the calling makes no sense.

Whether we agree or not with the conclusions that various preachers and writers draw from the Old Testament narratives, those narratives can be valuable sources for learning about God's ways. Also, we may wonder whether what God called people to do in Old Testament times was—with their limited knowledge—anything like what he asks of us now. Perhaps you, like I, have heard story sermons on, for example, the call of Moses or the call of Isaiah. But do we find any such calls in the New

Testament? (There will be more on that later.) So our question as to how God calls requires us to consider the purposes of God and the way he deals with his people in different times and circumstances. We can find parallels in the different ways God calls people to salvation.

There are striking, recent examples of God speaking to people who are totally unfamiliar with the Judeo-Christian tradition through dreams, as a preparation for the gospel. Sometimes, God has apparently caused a person to dream that a messenger would appear bringing a message that must be heeded. Within a short time, that person hears someone preaching the gospel or encounters somebody who brings a Christian witness. We are not accustomed to such things in our Western culture, though more so now among former Muslims.

Any call today issued by God is in the context of a larger calling to salvation and a holy life. This is especially important in our day of individualism. "How does God call me?" must be asked within the context "How does God call *us*?" And behind this question is the very nature of God as the one who calls. Frankly, a great deal of our conversation today about calling is centered on ourselves (and our desire for a deeper spiritual experience) rather than on the God who calls. To say this is by no means to minimize the importance of our hearing God, nor is it a minimizing of those who, like me, have preached and taught about such a close walk with God. It is rather to suggest that our highest quest should not be for guidance but for God himself.

**Second Question:** If there is such a thing as a call, how do I recognize it? No doubt many Christians have wished that they had the experience of the boy Samuel who heard God's voice clearly (1 Sam. 3), as we shall see in the following chapter. And we may envy the disciples who heard the audible voice of a visible Jesus calling them as, for examples, in Mark 3:13 and Luke 5:4–10. For most of us, there is no audible voice, and for none of us today is there an earthly Jesus. Therefore, we need to know how to discern when God is in fact directing us. Once again, the object of our inquiry is more than God's leading of us at various turns of our lives. And it is more than whether we should follow an inclination on our part to do or say something in a specific situation. We are focusing on that larger aspect of God's leading that involves vocational direction and perhaps a lifelong change that is fairly uniformly described as a call.

One problem is that not only have we been on the cusp of a major transition away from rationalism to postmodernism, but also we have recently seen a transition in the opposite direction from the rather subjective mind-set that characterized our immediately preceding generations with respect to a call. The idea of a call was thought by many to be an inner call that could not be rationalized. Consequently, some, at least, of the ministers and mission leaders of an older generation expected that a candidate for ordination or commissioning should testify to an inner persuasion that might not have supporting evidence. More recently, there has been a great emphasis on need, training, giftedness, and other factors. There has been, we might say, a *demystifying* of the call. So we may wonder whether the years ahead will witness a shift again toward a more inward recognition of a call with less rational consideration of outward circumstances and influences.

# 2

# What Does the Old Testament Teach about Calling?

In the Old Testament, God selected judges and prophets as well as others for particular spheres of service, but (perhaps surprisingly) the term *call* is usually not found in the actual accounts. Instead, there are other terms, as in Isaiah 61, where Isaiah said, "The Spirit of the Sovereign Lord is *on* me, because the Lord has *anointed* me, to *proclaim* good news to the poor. He has *sent* me ..." (v. 1).

What teachings and examples can help us understand calling? Our understanding will be enriched if we broaden our selection of passages beyond those that specifically use calling terminology. The creation account in Genesis 1 obviously lacks any instance of calling in the sense of a vocational summons; the Hebrew text uses the verb for call only in its sense of naming, not summoning. Our English idiom, to "call into being" might seem appropriate to describe God's verbal creative activity, but such calling terminology is not represented here. Yet God did speak the successive parts of his creation into being. In fact, the phrase "And God said" functions to introduce each section in the literary structure. This establishes God as the one who speaks and the one who creates, though not specifically as the one who calls. The passage introduces God as sovereign and omnipotent, whose spoken word is sufficient to bring into being the immense mass and energy in the universe, along with the sequence of events we know as time. Genesis 1 does not provide a theology of calling, but it does provide the foundation for such a theology in God's sovereignty and effective Word.

Chapters 2 and 3 of Genesis do not contain a call in the sense of God summoning people, but chapter 3 does describe a command (regarding the fruit of the tree) and its fateful rejection. As a result, God scolds Adam, "You listened to your wife." Listening would have been, and always is, the proper response to God's command, as it is to his call. Adam, however, responded to the wrong person, as had Eve. The result is a series of consequences that define future relational vocational assignments (family relationships and agriculture) in 3:16–19.

God continued to issue his commands to human beings, notably to Noah, and then he established his first covenant, also with Noah (Gen. 6–9). In these also, the initiative was the Lord's.

Moving ahead to Genesis 12, we see that the call of Abram, though not to a specific ministry or task, and without calling terminology, was certainly a sovereign, major, and definitive act of God in human history. It was a command of the sovereign God that left no uncertainty or room for negotiation. It required a major, massive move of Abram, his family, and his servants and animals—the entire entourage—to a distant and different land. It was a one-way, irreversible move that defined the history of that family, of the land to which they were sent, and of the millions of descendents, both physical and spiritual, down to the present day. However, in chapter 15:1, "The word of the Lord came to Abram in a vision." This word is important here because in the Old Testament, God's Word is not only informative; it is effective. Later, in chapter 22, God called Abraham (note the change from the name *Abram)* to offer his son, Isaac, as a sacrifice. Here also God was clearly the caller, without using calling language. But does Abraham's experience provide us with a mode for today? We must say no to that.

The saga of Joseph (Gen. 37–50) began not with a call from heaven but with fraternal conflict and the selling of the future hero into foreign hands. There was no summons for Joseph to acknowledge and obey. He did not choose his role. Nevertheless, the story concluded with what could be described as the Romans 8:28 of the Old Testament: Genesis 50:20. Joseph said to his brothers, "You intended to harm me, but God intended it for good."

Some four hundred years later, Moses' story began with a process of selection in which, because he was a baby, he also played no deliberate role. If there is an example here in these stories, it is of how God can accomplish his purposes in history without signaling the main players about them in advance.

Moses' experience was immensely important and theologically rich. God appeared to Moses within a burning bush and called to him. He revealed his name, spoke about the awful plight of his people in Egypt, and predicted his redemptive work there. But for our inquiry about calling and sending, we want to observe that God was sending Moses on a seemingly impossible mission. Exodus 3:10 records God's words. "I am sending you to Pharaoh." And in verse 14, God directed Moses to say to Pharaoh, "I AM has sent me to you." The importance of the sending resided in the transcendent glory of the immortal and powerful Sender. Obviously, the emphasis was not on a call but on the sending. Surely, that has significance for us today, as we shall come to see.

But there are at least two problems in finding a norm in this passage. One is that the appearance of the burning bush was unique. While we would be frightened by such a theophany, we would welcome some kind of sign that would validate what we might think is God's call to us. The other is that the word *call* does not occur in this passage. If we made it our goal to understand the ways God works to fulfill his purposes through his people, then the absence of a specific term, such as *call*, is not important. If we are looking for a specific experience or designation by God that is semantically designated as, and can technically be categorized as a call, then this can be disqualified. This immediately should warn us that perhaps we should be looking further for the "ways of God" in accomplishing his purposes through human beings. It suggests that we should be more concerned with the character of God and how he works and with the character of the person he chooses through whom to work, than with the specific means or terminology by which God calls that person.

The identification of Joshua as Moses' successor is strikingly different. Moses was designated as God's spokesperson and leader of his people; now the credentialing of the next person in that role was also done through Moses. It was, therefore, not necessary for Joshua himself to hear a voice from heaven. There were three steps in the transition of leadership. First, Moses, upon learning of his impending death, took the initiative to request God to appoint a successor (Num. 27:15-17). Second, God indicated who that successor would be (v. 18). Third, that individual was identified and commissioned in the presence of "the entire assembly" (v. 19).

The term translated "commissioned" (vv. 19, 23, *tsawah*) is so common in the Old Testament (504 occurrences) and used in so many different contexts with varying shades of meaning that it is precarious to offer a limited, technical, or specialized meaning here. Yet these varying uses and contexts usually relate to commanding someone, with a few meaning to put someone in command. (See 1 Chron. 22:12; Neh. 7:2) God's instructions to Moses included the following words in verse 20: "Give him some of your authority so the whole Israelite community will obey him." This prompts the reader to wonder what aspect or percentage of his authority Moses was to give to Joshua for Israel to obey. The Hebrew term translated "authority" (*hawadh*) conveys the idea of majesty. In Psalms 21:5 and 45:3, two typical examples, it is coupled with the term for "splendor," and in the former passage, it is parallel to "glory." So while the expected response to the majesty is obedience (v. 20 and v. 21b), which implies authority, there is an even grander aspect as the crowds recognized their new majestic leader. The bestowal of this majesty was accompanied by a literal hands-on indication of this transfer of leadership when Moses laid his hands on Joshua. "Now Joshua son of Nun was filled with the spirit of wisdom because (*ki*) Moses had laid his hands on him" (Deut. 34:9).

The crucial questions in the choice and appointment of Joshua are the following:

1. Whether it is an important example of calling
2. Whether it is in whole or in part intended to be a model, a pattern to be followed, and if that is the case
3. Whether it is a pattern that is valid beyond the Old Testament and for the church

Obviously, it is unique as to its historical setting and circumstances of Joshua's leadership. I propose that even without the specific terminology it was a calling, and that in the degenerate state of things in the period of judges, such a transition could not be repeated. So if it was a model, it was not so recognized.

There is an interesting contrast between the narratives about the beginnings of the ministry of the prophets Elijah and Elisha. The former person appears on the scene suddenly, giving God's word to King Ahab (1 Kings 1:1). Then God's word comes to Elijah in the form of a command, which Elijah proceeds to obey (vv. 2-6). There is no formal call. Elisha, on the other hand, is called by Elijah (1 Kings 19-21). This is an instance of what some term a "mediated call." In a mediated call, God calls the individual through someone else, whereas an immediate call, as the word suggests, is a call that God delivers directly to the person. But we must observe that in neither instance, that of Elijah or that of Elisha, do we encounter any call vocabulary.

Coming to the so-called Major Prophets, Isaiah's vision of the Lord "high and exalted" is truly awesome, and his hearing of the voice of the Lord is clearly described. "Whom shall I send? And who will go for us?" (Isa. 6:8) are words that speak to us across the intervening millennia. Several features of this narrative require our attention. One is that Isaiah's awareness of the exalted, sovereign Lord is basic to his mission. This is a principle we can surely carry over to our day and our experience. Another is the absence of call terminology. There is here, therefore, an essential principle to learn and follow, but not a formal structure that must be reproduced. A third feature is that the emphasis is not on Isaiah being designated to be a prophet but on Isaiah being sent on a mission to prophesy. We are going to see that this emphasis is relevant to New Testament practice and principle. We are not called to be elevated to some superior position. God calls us to be sent as servants on his mission.

So it is no surprise that in the latter part of Isaiah, we encounter the famous series of servant songs (e.g., Isa. 42:1-4; 44:1-5; 52:13-53:12). It is also significant that although we do not find the Hebrew word for "call" (*qara*) in the commission narratives about the prophets, it does occur in several servant songs. In these, *qara* is translated "called" or "chosen." "But you, O Israel, my servant, Jacob, whom I have chosen … I called you … I have chosen you" (Isa. 41:8-9) and "Here is my servant … I, the Lord, have called you in righteousness" (Isa. 42:1, 6;

see also 48:12, 15, 50:2), and the idea of calling by name in 43:1, 45:3). In the midst of these songs is a reference to the pagan king Cyrus, through whom God was going to accomplish the freeing of his people. God calls him his anointed and twice says that he summons Cyrus. Here in the word *summons* we do have calling terminology— and that is referring to a pagan! The effect is to establish in the reader's mind the fact of God's sovereignty over the nations and his particular care for his people, the descendents of Jacob (Israel) whom he has called.

Isaiah's experience is outstanding. If God employs a specialized appointment procedure that could be designated the call, why does calling terminology not occur in this historically prominent and significant event? Surely, it is not too demanding to expect that language. Furthermore, at this point in our inquiry, we should expect that if there is a procedure that can be described as the call, is it not strange that such terminology is also almost totally absent from the Bible? Our attempt to find a pattern of calling narratives in the Old Testament (and as we will see in the New Testament), has revealed more variety than uniformity.

The questions "Whom shall I send? And who will go for us?" (Isa. 6:8) in the context of the appearance of the exalted, sovereign Lord moved Isaiah to say, "Here I am, send me." This is the case also with Jeremiah and Ezekiel. They (and we) are not called to be elevated to some special position but to be sent as servants on a mission for the Lord. Once again, sending is more prominent than calling in what we name calling narratives.

Isaiah and Jeremiah had in common the fact that God sent them to bring his word to those who would not receive it (Isa. 6:8–10; Jer. 1:1–10). It is, therefore, understandable why the word of the Lord and Jeremiah's ability to speak it are so important in the opening of his book. He was "appointed as a prophet to the nations" (v. 5).

Ezekiel's personal experience was strikingly different, with visions of creatures and wheels (chapter 1). But in common with Isaiah, the emphasis is on God's word (1:3; 2:7) and on the prophet being sent (2:3, 4). We might have expected, if the basis on which a believer decides to commit his or her life to the Lord to serve him is a special experience of a call from God, that this would have certainly been true—and uniformly true-—of the prophets. Instead, as we have seen, it is not an experience of the prophet that validates his mission but the message itself, God's word.

For the Minor Prophets, there is nothing in the opening of Hosea about him being called, but we see the same theme of the word of the Lord coming to the prophet, who then is sent out with that word. This occurs in Hosea 1:1, 2; likewise, the word came to Joel (1:1). Amos was sent to prophesy, though he was not a prophet, bringing God's word to those who opposed the truth (Amos 7:14-17). Obadiah had a "message from the Lord" (1:1). So it is with the rest of the minor prophets, none of whom are said to be called but who did receive a word or oracle from the Lord. Clearly, the emphasis is on the coming of God's word to the prophets, and the importance of that word in the face of the defection of God's people and of the hostility of the pagan enemies.

Once again, the emphasis is not on an act of calling but the message itself, God's word.

There is one further bit of evidence that could be easily overlooked. Exodus 31 describes the work of Bezalel on the tabernacle. He was not a prophet or priest. He was in the building trades, or more accurately, he was a craftsman. Verse 2 tells us that God had chosen him. The word is *qara,* the simple word for "call." We might see little significance here, were it not that verse 3 informs us that the Lord told Moses that he had "filled him with the Spirit of God, with skill, ability, and knowledge in all kinds of crafts." So in order that we do not become elitist about God's call, we should remember that it is not only the prominent religious leader but also the devoted layperson who can be called by God and filled with the Spirit for his or her work.

Yet another consideration is that the commission narratives of the Old Testament were usually task specific. And the ministry of the prophets was not described as a call but as a mediation of the "word of the Lord." Thus, Haggai 1:1 describes that prophet's very limited focus. "In the second year of King Darius, on the first day of the sixth month, the word of the LORD came through the prophet Haggai to Zerubbabel son of Shealtiel, governor of Judah, and to Joshua son of Jehozadak, the high priest."

Does God call differently today? Are the Old Testament instances models for today? We must keep in mind that in several respects, the community of God's people in Old Testament times was not the same as the community of the early churches. The spiritual situation of Israel was different. The whole nation went through times of extreme idolatry and separation from God. Therefore, God had to call certain individuals one by one to govern, to lead the people back to himself, or to proclaim God's judgment. They lacked small communities of believers who could meet together seeking God's will and who then communicated his leading to individuals God wanted to lead into special ministries. After the Moses-Joshua continuum, God had to work, so to speak, directly from heaven. The rulers were for the most part inept, if not evil. The people who might have maintained spiritual continuity usually needed to hear God's word through someone he chose (called?) as a messenger. Think of the circumstances in the time of Isaiah, Jeremiah, Hosea, Nehemiah, and so on.

Also, the social structure was different. There were no communities equivalent in structure to our local churches. The synagogue was a post-exilic development. It is also difficult to conceive of how God could have called a Moses during his exile other than by direct communication. The burning bush was not a model for the divine call. It was the appropriate means to a man in the desert, hundreds of miles from his people. Jeremiah wept over the sin of his people. He could not have been designated by some group of believers as a prophet. Isaiah was singled out by God in a marvelous way and told to speak to people who would not hear him. He also could not have expected to be called by such people.

Now we come to the question: are these examples of calling in the Old Testament valid for today? This question is not easy to answer. Outstanding characters clearly received orders from God to do remarkable exploits. But specific calling terminology is almost absent from the biblical narratives where we would expect it. Therefore, wonderful as the commission narratives of the Old Testament were, and instructive as they are for our own sensitivity to God and his leading, they should not lead us to expect a direct, tangible call from God. While God is certainly able to do this when he so chooses, it is not the norm in the Old Testament, and especially not in the New Testament.

# 3

# What Is Distinctive about Calling in the New Testament?

## The Disciples

A passage that is very relevant to our questions about calling is Mark 3:13-19, where Jesus appoints his disciples. This is a significant narrative in the New Testament, where the word *call* occurs in a direct person-to-person conversation. The following elements in the narrative have bearing on the issue of calling:

> Jesus went up on a mountainside and called to him those he wanted. He appointed twelve that they might be with him and that he might send them out to preach and to have authority to drive out demons. These are the twelve he appointed: Simon (to whom he gave the name Peter), James son of Zebedee and his brother John (to them he gave the name Boanerges, which means "sons of thunder"), Andrew, Philip,

> Bartholomew, Matthew, Thomas, James son of Alphaeus, Thaddaeus, Simon the Zealot and Judas Iscariot, who betrayed him.

He is sovereign; he makes the choice. "And they came to him." They responded. Apart from Judas Iscariot, there was no resistance, as far as we know. "He appointed twelve—designating them apostles." Three verbs have been used so far: *call*, *appoint*, and *designate*. Although we should probably be right in assuming that the first two verbs could apply to any of us, only the Twelve received this particular designation as apostles.

We observe that Jesus deals with his disciples regarding their commission both individually and corporately. In Luke's narrative of Jesus' calling of Peter individually, there follows a miraculous catch of fish (Luke 5:5–7). An extreme example of individualization occurs at the end of John's gospel when Jesus tells Peter that his plans for another disciple (probably John) are none of Peter's business (John 21:20-21). Another observation (also in Luke) is that the commission Jesus gives to the fishermen is couched in terms of fishing. They are thrust into eternal kingdom business for the Son of God now to be fishers of men, a carryover from their secular vocation of fishing. A third is that a call or commission from the Lord can be given in stages or perhaps repeated, without any implication that this is because of any lack of spirituality on the part of the disciples (with the exception of Peter's confirmation of his call after his denial of Christ).

Fourth, calling is conditioned on obedience. "Because you say so I will let down the nets" (Luke 5:5). The

specific commission was "That they might be with him."
This is the heart of discipleship and the main purpose of
God's call. "And that he might send them out to preach" is
a second goal. We know from the larger context that this
has to do with announcing the impending kingdom and
proclaiming the King. Preaching involved an itinerant life
at great cost for the sake of Christ. One reason for this
(as the text in Mark implies) is the intense, crucial, and
dangerous ministry that we often call spiritual warfare.
Jesus' own ministry involved considerable conflict
with evil spirits. He, and the disciples acting under his
authority, assaulted the kingdom of evil and drove out the
very demons that were Satan's offensive line.

"When Jesus had called the Twelve together, he
gave them power and authority to drive out all demons
and to cure diseases, and he sent them out to proclaim
the kingdom of God and to heal the sick." With this
commission, Jesus called his disciples to a conflict. His own
ministry involved considerable conflict with opponents. It
is significant that in this passage, the reference to authority
occurs not in the phrase about preaching but in the phrase
about driving out demons.

Too often today, preachers think of authority as some
superior position or right they have over the congregation.
Some may forget that authority in preaching derives from
the Word of God, not from their opinions. But even
beyond that concern, we must recognize the significance
of the fact that in this passage in Mark, the reference to
authority concludes *not* in the phrase about preaching
but in the phrase about *driving out demons*. This is also the
case in Luke 9:1. The operative word in both passages

is *sent,* not *called.* The case is the same in Luke 10:1. "After this the Lord appointed seventy-two others and *sent* them two by two ahead of him to every town and place where he was about to go." We cannot expect to receive a call from God—whatever that may mean—if we are not willing to be obedient disciples. Being a disciple of Jesus means following Jesus. Responding to a call is impossible without following the one who calls. Later on, Jesus interacts strongly with people who want to follow him on their own terms and without cost (Luke 9:57-62).

We also saw above that the call received by all believers is to holy fellowship with God. Now we see that the call received by the Twelve in particular was to fellowship with Jesus. Even for those who are not apostles, the principle must undoubtedly apply that we should not seek a calling from the Lord to go *out* for him unless we desire first of all to come to be *with* him.

We have been using the term *call* throughout this section, but (with one exception) the term itself is *not* used in the narratives mentioned so far. The exception is Matthew 4:21, another passage about Jesus selecting his disciples. Bibles that have section titles typically have something like "Jesus Calls His Disciples" for verses 18-22. The justification for that is in verse 21, which concludes with the words "Jesus called them" (the sons of Zebedee). The term *called* here seems to be used in an ordinary sense. One can picture Jesus standing on the shore calling out to them. How else could he get their attention? It is only if we approach the text with the presumption that calling is a specific, technical term for an appointment to ministry that we would see it here.

Could the absence of the word *calling* in that assumed special sense mean, therefore, that calling is *not* an appropriate term for God's selection of people to serve him? The first is in the ordinary sense of summoning or asking someone to come over to be with you. If that is the case, it is inconsequential with respect to the specialized kind of calling we are considering. This conclusion would be fortified by the fact noted above that when Mark describes the actual commissioning of the disciples he does *not* describe this as a call. A logical (and theological) application of this passage is that in the context of today's church, a person who feels called to preach should, rather than setting out alone, be sent by the church.

However, we are also called to follow Jesus as our example. "To this you were called, because Christ suffered for you, leaving you an example" (1 Peter 2:21); "That you may know the hope to which he has called you" (Eph. 1:18); "Called to share in the glory of our Lord Jesus Christ" (2 Thess. 2:14); "Called to his eternal glory in Christ" (1 Peter 5:10); "Our knowledge of him who called us" (2 Peter 1:3); "Peace ... called to peace" (Col. 3:15); "The eternal life to which you were called" (1 Tim. 6:12); "And the 'prize' for which God has called me heavenward" (Phil. 3:14).

## Paul

Is there any instance in the New Testament of a clear calling to a specific ministry? The experience of Paul at his conversion is well known (Acts 9:1-19), but it is not until Acts 13:2 that the text tells us clearly that he was called to a specific work. The initial words to Paul were not "You are called" but "Why do you persecute me?" Paul's reaction was not "Please use me" but "Who are you, Lord?" And the response was that Jesus identifies himself and says, "Now get up and go into the city and you will be told what you must do." God directed him to where he would meet Ananias, whom he prepared for this meeting with Paul. Ananias was told, "Go! This man is my chosen instrument to proclaim my name to the Gentiles and their kings and to the people of Israel ... I will show him how much he must suffer for my name" (v. 15). The word *calling* does not appear anywhere in the narrative.

The three accounts of Paul's conversion on the road to Damascus provide us with an expanded sequence of events that are important with regard to Paul's call. The account does not, however, tell us anything specific that Ananias said to Paul about his mission or suffering. In Paul's own description of the events to the people in Jerusalem, he states that when the Lord spoke to him from heaven, he said, "Go into Damascus. There you will be told all you are assigned to do" (Acts 22:10). So the initial word from heaven was to be supplemented by further instructions, which we know (from chapter 9) that Ananias gave to Paul. Paul's account during his trial before Agrippa (Acts 26:12-18) makes no mention of this supplementary commission. The purpose there was to enlarge on the words from heaven, specifically about turning the Gentiles to God.

Paul was called both to preach and to be an apostle. In Galatians 1:15, Paul states that God set him apart from birth and "called me by his grace, was pleased to reveal his Son in me so that I might preach him among the Gentiles." The use of the word *called* here is somewhat ambiguous. On the one hand, it could refer to Paul's salvation, but on the other hand, the purpose clause "so that I might preach him among the Gentiles" makes it more likely that this is God's calling to apostleship. Furthermore, while the terminology "called by his grace" sounds purely soteriological, Paul's autobiographical comments in 1 Timothy 1:12-17, which also speak of God's grace to him (vv. 12-15), are related to his being appointed "to [God's] service" (v. 12), all of which is to God's glory (v. 17). When this is linked to the idea of Paul's being "set apart from birth," the language of consecration as well as salvation, we see the whole religious connotation and God's purpose in Paul's calling. This should be read in connection with Romans 1:1—"Paul called to be an apostle and set apart for the gospel of God"—and 1 Corinthians 1:1, which says, "Paul called an apostle." Add to this Paul's description of the Roman believers as "among those who are called to belong to Jesus Christ" (Rom. 1:6), and we see the broader setting. All believers are called to a relationship with Christ and to a holy life that is consecrated to God. Paul's calling had a unique dimension in that he was an apostle.

The word *apostle* has significance in view of the language that was used in Judaism and early Christianity to describe special emissaries. Also, as is often pointed out, the related Greek verb *apostello* means "send," not "call." It is important to note that the words *appoint, designate,* and *apostles* place the emphasis not on calling but on sending in this significant passage. The specific purpose for the appointment was first "that they might be with him." This is the heart of discipleship and the main purpose of God's calling, as we have already seen in various biblical texts. We noted that the larger call, which extends to all believers, is to a holy fellowship with God. Here we see that call focused on the Twelve in their relationship with Jesus. If we expect to do great things for God and invest hours weekly in service, but are not interested and prepared to spend hours in fellowship with him, we have misunderstood his call. If we do not love him supremely, we need not apply for the shepherd's position.

In his writings, Paul identifies himself as a servant and an apostle (Rom. 1:1; 1 Cor. 1:1; 2 Cor. 1:1; Gal. 1:1; Eph. 1:1; Phil. 1:1 [along with Timothy], Col. 1:1; 1 Tim. 1:1; 2 Tim. 1:1). In Philemon 1:1, he calls himself "a prisoner of Christ Jesus," along with Timothy. In 1 and 2 Thessalonians, he simply puts his and Timothy's names, and in 1 and 2 Timothy, that person is considered to be his son.

If there is anyone in the New Testament who deserves to be identified as called, it is Paul. Yet in Romans 8:37, Paul said, "We are more than conquerors through him who *loved* us," not "called us." Earlier in the chapter, he lists himself among those who are called (v. 30), and in verse 33, he is among those who are chosen. As it is, the term must be an optional designation of all those in the body of Christ. Our task is to see what special description or benefit it has for all believers.

We might have thought that Paul, with his mighty gifts, zeal, and personal devotion to the Lord, would strike out on his own to evangelize the world. Instead, Acts 13 finds him among a group of church leaders who were prophesying and teaching and, as the narrative opens, fasting and praying. "While they were worshiping the Lord and fasting, the Holy Spirit said, 'Set apart for me Barnabas and Saul for the work to which I have called them.' So after they had fasted and prayed, they placed their hands on them and sent them off" (Acts 13:2). The background of this commissioning is that God first led Barnabas through the church at Jerusalem to go to Antioch. His ministry there was effective and his character was demonstrated (Acts 11:22-24). Next Barnabas looked for Saul and brought him to Antioch, where the two taught the Antioch church for a year (11:25, 26). There is nothing said of a call or spiritual leading in these two verses; the action is described in an almost matter-of-fact way. The two men (with Barnabas still named first) were then sent to Judea with help for an impending famine, predicted by the prophet Agabus. It is striking that although their going to Antioch to teach had been described matter-of-factly, what seems as a more human, practical mission—taking famine aid—was prompted by a special prediction from the Holy Spirit (11:27-30).

The calling of Barnabas and Saul, therefore, was a work of the Holy Spirit, accomplished through the church. We must always be careful, lest we change the simple description of an event in Acts to a prescription of what we must do today. But with that caution in mind, we can say that if there is any model or pattern of calling in the book of Acts, it is this. It involves the Holy Spirit (whose call is clear), the church, and the individual. This is significantly different from the pattern that is often seen today: an individual (who either is certain that the Holy Spirit is leading or is seeking certainty) and the church (which may or may not have been consulted in the discerning process), which is asked for support.

The two men had already been in Christian service, and their commission now was not to a life of ministry but to a specific work, which surprisingly turns out to have been just one missionary journey of limited duration. Acts 14:26 specifically and unambiguously calls it completed. "From Attalia they sailed back to Antioch where they had been committed to the grace of God for the work they had now completed." For that purpose, they fasted and prayed, placed their hands on them, and "sent them off." Placing hands on someone was a common action with various meanings, including the public designation of a successor as we have already seen in the case of Joshua. It could also symbolize (or be the actual means of) the transmission of a spiritual gift, as was the case when Paul himself and the elders of an unspecified church placed hands on Timothy. (See below.)

Putting all this together, we see that, just as in Paul's words in Galatians 1:15-16, there is a blending here of Paul's call to conversion and his call to preach to Jews and Gentiles. Significantly, however, the second phase of his calling did not come only from heaven. God chose to confirm that call through Ananias, and we infer that this confirmation included further details especially about the suffering Paul would have to endure.

How does all this help us as we seek an understanding as to what we should expect in terms of a call from God today? First, we always need to keep in mind that Paul was an apostle. That means that some of his experiences, and especially the God-given authority that Paul claimed and exercised, were unique and not for all Christians. Second, we see that even Paul, the great apostle, needed to hear his commission affirmed and apparently enlarged upon by another believer, Ananias, who was already a disciple and through whom God chose to mediate his call to Paul.

Does Romans 10 describe a specific call to preaching? The famous missionary passage in Romans 10:11-15 vividly employs calling terminology, but perhaps surprisingly, not in connection with preaching.

> As Scripture says, "Anyone who believes in him will never be put to shame" for there is no difference between Jew and Gentile— the same Lord is Lord of all and richly blesses all who call on him, for 'Everyone who calls on the name of the Lord will be saved. How, then, can they call on the one they have not believed in? And how can they believe in the one of whom they have not heard? And how can they hear without someone preaching to them? And how can anyone preach unless they are sent? As it is written: "How beautiful are the feet of those who bring good news!"

The point is clear. God wants people to call on him, but for that to happen, they need to hear about him. This requires that messengers be sent to preach the gospel. Having used the word *call* three times with reference to people calling on the Lord, we might have reason to expect that Paul would, as a rhetorical device, use the same word reciprocally in connection with preachers. However, the key word here is *sent*, not *called*. While calling is not ruled out, neither is it expressed. Therefore, if we are going to be strictly faithful to the biblical text, the passage cannot be offered as evidence of a special call to preaching.

Another aspect of God's call is the call to be saints. "To all in Rome who are loved by God and called to be saints" (Rom. 1:7); "To the church of God in Corinth … called to be holy, together with all those everywhere who call on the name …" (1 Cor. 1:2). This is above all a "holy calling." "Who has saved us and called us to a holy life" (2 Tim. 1:9); "For God did not call us to be impure, but to live a holy life" (1 Thess. 4:7); "Just as he who called you is holy, so be holy in all you do" (1 Peter 1:15).

# What Can We Learn from 1 Corinthians?

The introduction in 1 Corinthians 1:2 to this theme of holy character leads to a strong reemphasis and further explanation of God's calling in the body of that epistle. The word *calling* is especially prominent in the first chapter of 1 Corinthians (vv. 1, 2, 9, 24, 26). All of the believers at Corinth, however immature they may have been, and however much inclined to fulfill their own desires, had been called by God. This parallels their spiritual giftedness (1:4–9). Their blessedness in being called and gifted makes their immaturity and tolerance of sin all the more unconscionable. But though they had not properly fulfilled their calling, the *fact* of their calling remained. In the opening of the letter, Paul first affirms his own calling to be an apostle. This authorized him to declare God's will to the errant Corinthian church. Verse 2 declares that they were "called to be his holy people," a striking application of what we observed above regarding our calling to be a holy people. This is a double affirmation, as they were both "sanctified in Christ Jesus" and "called to be saints."

In the same sentence, Paul writes of "all those everywhere who call on the name of our Lord Jesus Christ (1 Cor. 1:2)." Calling terminology is on his mind, but not only the terminology of a call to ministry. Paul is stressing the importance of our character and relationship to the Lord, and in verse 9, he says God has "called you into fellowship with his Son Jesus Christ our Lord." When he comes to verse 24, he uses the word *call* absolutely; that is, without reference to that to which one is called. It is clear that "to those whom God has called, both Jew and Greeks," refers to their call to salvation as they came to know "Christ the power of God and wisdom of God." Immediately after that, in verse 26, Paul urges the Corinthians to "think of what you were when you were called," again a reference of their calling to salvation. This reference to the point of their salvation as their calling is picked up in chapter 7, where Paul urges his readers not to think that becoming Christians meant that they must make immediate changes in their personal and vocational circumstances (vv. 17, 18, 20, 21, 24). He did, however, advise those whose marriage was threatened by an unbelieving spouse that they should not fight to preserve a marriage characterized by conflict, because "God has called us to live in peace" (7:15). This chapter teaches both that God calls people while they are *in* various circumstances (as in verse 20, "when God called him") and that God calls people *to* various circumstances (as in verse 17, "to which God has called" them).

Returning to 1 Corinthians 1, we observe that when Paul writes about the differences between the opponents of Christ and the gospel, who use rhetorical and other skills that the Christians lacked, he adds choosing terminology to his calling terminology. Believers, who may seem foolish in their simplicity, but those who know the power and wisdom that is in the gospel of Christ, are the very ones whom God has called. God actually "chose the foolish things of the world to shame the wise; God chose the weak things of the world to shame the strong. God chose the lowly things of this world and the despised things—and the things that are not—to nullify the things that are, so that no one may boast before him" (1:27–29). Here a purpose is expressed, the honoring of God by his using those of low status in the world's eyes to bring down those of high status. The action depicted is not God calling individuals to a particular ministry but God choosing an assortment of people to become believers and become engaged in a great ministry: evangelism. This broadens the field of those who serve the Lord. God calls, and he receives glory not only through those who are specially gifted and trained but also through those are not. The point is made again in verse 31, which says, "Therefore, as it is written: 'Let the one who boasts boast in the Lord.'"

Now Paul introduces an observation that may come as a surprise. In spite of this expansive treatment of the theme of calling, and in spite of the reference to Paul's calling to be an apostle, there is no teaching in 1 Corinthians that Christians need or receive any special calling to church ministry. It is too soon to draw any conclusions from this observation. There are a number of examples of what we would describe as calling in both Old Testament and New Testament. We need great care in examining these examples, and we must realize that what is needed today is not a deconstruction of the passages but an understanding of the term *calling*. That is, we accept and understand the passages as they stand and let them define or redefine our common but ambiguous term *calling*. This is done rather than imposing on them a fabric of calling terminology that we ourselves have woven. We need to ask if the mystery in calling simply lies in assumptions about our common use of the term. Perhaps we can construct a better vocabulary, a carefully distinguished set of terms that conform better to the biblical evidence. This vocabulary will need not only to conform to passages about calling but also function in accordance with the larger group of passages about sending.

A very helpful way of considering the vocabulary of calling in the New Testament is to read the verses in groups. The first of these describes the power of the gospel. Matthew 9:13 (cf. Mk. 2:17 and 1 Cor. 1:26–31) portrays the condition of those who were called. The first employs the word *sinners.* "I have not come to call the righteous, but sinners" (Matt. 9:13, Mark 2:17). "Brothers and sisters, think of what you were when you were called" (1 Cor. 1:26). It offers an admission of guilt. No one can claim to be called without that.

In 1 Corinthians 1:26–29, the word *chosen* also serves to identify the called.

> Brothers and sisters, think of what you were when you were called. Not many of you were wise by human standards; not many were influential; not many were of noble birth. But God chose the foolish things of the world to shame the wise; God chose the weak things of the world to shame the strong. God chose the lowly things of this world and the despised things—and the things that are not—to nullify the things that are, so that no one may boast before him.

These people had much to remember. They were brought to Christ by Paul, who himself was "called to be an apostle" (1 Cor. 1:1). Those who heard this letter read to them knew it had come from the apostle who first brought them the saving gospel. They were "sanctified in Christ Jesus and called to be his holy people" (1:2). They now were in a fellowship with "all those everywhere who call on the name of our Lord Jesus Christ—their Lord and ours." Calling is mentioned three times in the first three verses, hardly an accident. This is followed by a further thanksgiving and is concluded by the happy confirmation "God is faithful, who has called you into fellowship with his Son, Jesus Christ our Lord" (1:9). This echoes Isaiah 49:7, which concludes with a reference to "the Lord, who is faithful, the Holy One of Israel, who has chosen you."

Verses 22-25 between these two sections of chapter 1 in 1 Corinthians remind them and us that we are called to testify to God's wisdom and power:

> Jews demand signs and Greeks look for wisdom, but we preach Christ crucified: a stumbling block to Jews and foolishness to Gentiles, but to those whom God has called, both Jews and Greeks, Christ the power of God and the wisdom of God. For the foolishness of God is wiser than human wisdom, and the weakness of God is stronger than human strength.

We have seen that a number of verses assure us that we have been called to a holy life. Two of these occur together, Romans 1:6 and 7. "And you also are among those Gentiles who are called to belong to Jesus Christ" (Rom. 1:6). "To all in Rome who are loved by God and called to be his holy people" (Rom. 1:7). These verses express two relationships, to Christ and to God. The first is simple belonging; the second expresses a change on our part, "to be his holy people."

It is not possible to respond to God's call without experiencing a transformation. God's call to salvation is at the same time a call to change our lifestyle. But also the object of our life undergoes transformation. "I pray also that the eyes of your heart may be enlightened in order that you may know the hope to which he has called you, the riches of his glorious inheritance in his holy people, and his incomparably great power for us who believe" (Eph. 1:18-19).

Our eyes are now turned to heaven. "I press on toward the goal to win the prize for which God has called me heavenward in Christ Jesus" (Phil. 3:14). The word *glory* now appears. "He called you to this through our gospel, that you might share in the glory of our Lord Jesus Christ" (2 Thess. 2:14). "And the God of all grace, who called you to his eternal glory in Christ, after you have suffered a little while, will himself restore you and make you strong, firm and steadfast. To him be the power forever and ever. Amen" (1 Peter 5:10-11). "His divine power has given us everything we need for life and godliness through our knowledge of him who called us by his own glory and goodness" (2 Peter 1:3).

This leads to, "Fight the good fight of the faith. Take hold of the eternal life to which you were called when you made your good confession in the presence of many witnesses" (1 Tim. 6:12). Our life together is described by the word *peace.* "Let the peace of Christ rule in your hearts, since as members of one body you were called to peace. And be thankful" (Col. 3:15). We can confirm our calling. "Therefore, my brothers and sisters, make every effort to confirm your calling and election. For if you do these things, you will never fall and you will receive a rich welcome into the eternal kingdom of our Lord and

Savior Jesus Christ" (2 Peter 1:10-11). The contribution of 1 Corinthians is wonderful. Standing by itself, it calls for an entire response to the experience of the believer.

## The Experience of Timothy

Timothy's experience is important for us because he is the only individual whom the New Testament specifically identifies as having been both singled out and gifted for ministry, and he receives two letters giving instructions for his ministry. Just prior to the account of Paul's selection of Timothy, Paul and Barnabas had chosen Silas and Mark, respectively, as their companions (Acts 15:36-41). This was after Mark had left the missionary group, Paul having been unwilling to have him as an associate. There is no reference in the New Testament to a prior calling or other introduction of either Silas or Mark to a life of ministry. In Timothy's case he seems to have been first chosen by Paul in Acts 16:1-3 when Paul visited Lystra and then was later spiritually gifted in some way when Paul and a group of elders laid their hands on him (1 Tim. 4:14; 2 Tim. 1:6). Also in 2 Timothy, 1:6 Paul writes him "to fan into flame the gift of God, which is in you through the laying on of my hands. For God did not give us a spirit of timidity, but a spirit of power, of love and of self-discipline." So the gift, which is related to the spirit (or Spirit) in 2 Timothy, was given, according to 1 Timothy, when hands were laid on him. With Timothy, there was apparently some reluctance on the part of the Christians to respect his leadership, so a reference to the visible declaration of his calling was necessary.

The term *called* is never applied to Timothy. This is somewhat surprising, as we might have expected that a person as important as he would have been so designated. The instructions of 1 Timothy 4:12-16, including "Set an example … Do not neglect your gift … Watch your life and doctrine closely," may take the place of *called*. But if so, the complete omission of that term might show its unimportance. The same could be said of 2 Timothy 1:16, which says, "For this reason I remind you to fan into flame the gift of God, which is in you through the laying on of my hands." Does the laying on of hands replace calling? I think it does. Furthermore, the laying on of hands eventually gives way to group decisions and the decisions of leaders.

What do we learn then from his experience? It is perplexing that the book of Acts does not feature individuals receiving a special call to ministry or missions after the time of Christ. The Lord Jesus personally called his twelve disciples and then, speaking directly from heaven, personally called Paul. After that, the norm seems to be that the church and its leaders are the agents of God in transmitting his call. That does not mean that the Spirit of God does not move in an individual's life, leading her or him to special service. An inner call is certainly always an option for the sovereign God to choose, and God's servants down through the centuries give ample testimony to such a sense of calling. But the New Testament narrative in Acts suggests that God moves through the church and its leaders to give or to confirm his special call.

There will always be individuals who rise up with fire in their hearts to serve their Lord, but the individualism that has so often characterized at least American Christianity does not seem to be the way of the early church. Theirs was a corporate life in which all believers were to function and flourish. Any misunderstandings of God's leading, perhaps distorted by subjectivism or personal sins of pride or overconfidence, could be identified by the body of believers and corrected.

In short, God's call, however strongly felt by the individual, should also be heard and confirmed by the church.

# 4

# Sending: A Step beyond Calling

If you pay any attention to Chicago politics, it is easy to be simultaneously fascinated and repulsed. There is a story from the late forties about Abner Mikva who went on to become a famous Illinois congressman and a federal judge. While in law school, the story goes, he walked into an Illinois Democratic committeeman's office to volunteer as a campaign worker. The committeeman eyed him suspiciously and asked him "Who sent you?" He answered, "Nobody." The committeeman said, "We don't want nobody nobody sent." Nor does the church, or for that matter, the world, easily accept someone who has no credentials, no one to vouch for them, no guarantee that what they say is dependable. When the stakes are so high—eternal life or death—it becomes infinitely more important (no exaggeration) that someone who claims spiritual authority and a valid claim to speak truth has a sender behind them. In both church and secular society, we often use the term *called* to describe the motivation that thrusts a person into a challenging situation. But what if only that solitary person hears the call? Do we invoke the familiar image of a tree falling in a forest with no one there to hear: Was there really a sound?

Undoubtedly, most Christians have at some time wished that Jesus were present in person to solve a problem or give them advice. This is probably the case with calling and sending. It was all so clear in the gospel narrative. "Jesus called to him those he wanted … he appointed twelve." There was no uncertainty. They knew who they were. How can we apply the way Jesus called and sent out his disciples to our situation today? Over the centuries, Christians have tried to make Jesus contemporary. In recent times, we have had red-letter editions of the New Testament to make Jesus' words stand out. For a while, it was popular to have WWJD bracelets to prompt the wearers to ask, "What would Jesus do?" Jesus' parables are retold in modern language and circumstances to make them contemporary. Those who feel called to serve God in some specific way would like to have his unambiguous affirmation. When that calling eventuates in the fearsome reality of leaving familiar territory to begin a new assignment we believe is his will, the voice and hand of Jesus himself would bring great encouragement.

*Sending is the complement of calling.* Like calling, it is a sovereign act of God to accomplish his purposes through men and women. We sometimes think of the sending of a missionary as a parallel to the appointment of an ambassador. That is valid, but only to an extent. As for the simple validity of the parallel, ambassadors are appointed and sent; missionaries are called and sent. In both cases, the individual is responsible to represent the sender faithfully. Another parallel is even closer. This is from the early centuries after Christ, recorded in the Jewish Talmud. It is a narrative about one rabbi sending another rabbi on a mission. When the traveler arrives at his destination, he delivers the following instructions from the sender regarding the reception he should be given: "Receive him as myself." We are often reminded that the word *apostle* derives from the Greek noun *apostolos*, which is related to the verb *apostello*, "I send."

We need to realize that Christian apostles did not only convey a message; there was a sense in which they *were* the message. Paul's words concerning his reception at Thessalonica are vividly descriptive. "You know how we lived among you ... [people] report what kind of reception you gave us ... The appeal we make does not spring from error or impure motives ... We speak as men approved by God entrusted with the gospel ... When you received the Word of God, which you heard from us, you accepted it not as the word of men but as it actually is the Word of God" (1 Thess. 1:5, 9; 2:3, 4, 13). Paul's life was part of his message. For the Lord's apostles, those who are sent represent the Lord who is sending them. What then is the mode of sending today? Does God send people in obedience to what seems to be his call and direction? Or is this in some way mediated or discerned by a body of believers?

It has been common in recent years to apply the term *incarnational* to the witness of believers. Christ became flesh, his incarnation (from the Latin *in* and a form of *carnis,* "flesh"). After the resurrection and ascension of Christ (or, as some would put it, "after the days of his flesh," the Holy Spirit reproduces, as it were, the person of Christ in the believer—in our flesh. So the risen Christ lives by the Holy Spirit in us to bring Christ wherever we go. He is seen in our lives, our love, and our service. Being *sent* is, however, a significant step beyond that. There were many people in Galilee who loved Jesus and could give "a cup of cold water" in his name. Some submitted themselves as his followers and accepted the conditions of discipleship, even to the point of selling what they had and giving to the poor, as Jesus taught. But not all of them were among those who were specially sent, like the group of twelve apostles and the group of seventy (in Luke 10). In fact, we know of one who wanted to go with the Lord but was not accepted as his disciple (Luke 9:61-62), and of another who also asked to go with him but was told to stay and be a witness where he was (Luke 8:38-39). Likewise, after Jesus' resurrection, many in Asia Minor, Greece, and Rome came to love Christ the Lord and brought others to faith in him. But in the narrative of Acts, Paul called specific individuals to work with him and sent them on missions. We immediately think of Timothy and Titus, but others were named in Paul's letters. We will explore both Old Testament and New Testament examples to discern how this sending applies to our twenty-first-century lives and circumstances.

## Old Testament

The words *send* and *sent* are so common in both the Old Testament and New Testament that any attempt to screen out the religious from the secular uses of the term and provide a listing of these is far beyond what we need for our purposes. Beginning with the Old Testament, we will cite some significant examples to provide a landscape against which we can portray the act of sending in its relation to God's call.

Instead of the calling terminology that we might have expected in the narrative of Moses and the burning bush, another term appears: *sending*. In Exodus 3:10, God says to Moses, "So now go. I am sending you to Pharaoh to bring my people the Israelites out of Egypt." The verb is repeated several times. God says, "And this will be the sign that it is I who have sent you" (v. 12). Moses asks, "Suppose I go … and say to them 'The God of your fathers has sent me to you'" (v. 13). Moses is to say, "I AM has sent me to you" (v. 14) and "The Lord, the God of your fathers … has sent me to you" (v. 15). The cluster of sending verbs in Exodus 3 occurs within a typical Hebrew structure of narrative repetition. The function of the verb *send* is to emphasize that Moses is not acting on his own authority; he is responsible to God and the people are responsible to hear God's message through Moses. In chapter 4, it occurs again, this time not for emphasis but in Moses' remonstrance, of a sort often found in calling narratives, "Lord, please send someone else" (4:13).

However, Moses' uneasiness reappears after the golden calf incident. He says to God, "You have been telling me, 'Lead these people,' but you have not let me know whom you will send with me" (Ex. 33:12). After God assures Moses of his continuing presence, Moses responded, "If your presence does not go with us, do not send us up from here" (v. 15). Obviously, in those circumstances, there was no human institution or organization that was in a position to send Moses. God had to do that directly. (The same was true during the disorganized time of the judges. See Judges 6:14.)

An important instance of God's acts of sending occurs in Exodus 23:20-21.

> See, I am sending an angel ahead of you to guard you along the way and to bring you to the place I have prepared. Pay attention to him and listen to what he says. Do not rebel against him; he will not forgive your rebellion, since my Name is in him.

The people were to recognize and obey the divine presence in that angel. God promised to send also his terror ahead of them and confuse the opposing nations (v. 27). Given the parallel language, the terror, like the angel, represents God's own presence. In Exodus 33:2, God also promises to send an angel to do battle for them. While this, of course, does not provide us with a model that is pertinent to humans, it shows us how God works in human affairs through his emissaries. Perhaps the best-known instance of this is the sending of Gabriel to the Virgin Mary to announce the coming birth of Jesus. The sovereign Lord of the universe accomplishes his purposes through both human and super-human beings. He can also speak through figures in dreams, as apparently many Muslim and others today are experiencing in preparation for their hearing the gospel through the human being that figure represents. Ultimately, however, God sends people to proclaim the gospel.

Further instances of sending occur in the Old Testament historical books, some more striking than others. In the opening events of Joshua, the "Reubenites, the Gadites and the half-tribe of Manasseh tell Joshua that they will obey what he commands and go where he sends them, making it clear that they consider Joshua to be acting on God's behalf just as Moses was" (Josh. 1:16-18). When an angel of the Lord approaches Gideon, he asks why the Lord seems to have abandoned the Israelites. "The Lord turned to him and said, 'Go in the strength you have … Am I not sending you?'" (Judg. 6:14). When the sins of King Saul necessitated choosing a successor, the Lord spoke to Samuel the prophet and said, "I am sending you to Jesse of Bethlehem. I have chosen one of his sons to be king." The use of the word *send* might seem ordinary if it were not that the provision of David as king is of immense importance in the history of Israel. It took the direct action of God by sending Samuel to achieve that succession of kingship.

These examples demonstrate the active involvement of the sovereign God in the direction of his people. We may wonder how this information was conveyed to the individuals who were sent and how they knew their assignment. That is not an issue in the case of a divine messenger, of course, and in the case of Moses, his entire conversation was with the God who made his immediate presence known through the burning bush. In other instances, however, the mode of communication is not clear.

One of the frequently quoted passages of Scripture during missionary exhortations is Isaiah 6:1-13, especially verse 8. "Then I heard the voice of the Lord saying,

'Whom shall I send? And who will go for us?' And I said, 'Here am I. Send me!'" The word *send* is prominent, and the word *go* stands in parallel to it in a command/obedience sequence. It should probably be described as a commissioning rather than just as a calling narrative that happens to lack specific calling terminology. God does not initiate the conversation by simply drawing Isaiah into conversation, as we might expect in a call narrative, but by dramatically confronting him with his holiness, causing Isaiah to recoil in confession of guilt. But immediately God closes the gap between them by the act of cleansing. Only then is Isaiah prepared to hear the commission "Go!" At that point, God describes the impossibility of Isaiah's task. His response is not to question, protest, or claim inability. The conversation ends without further interaction.

Although we would probably like assurance of a personal assignment directly from God, few of us would relish being faced in our sinful state by the holy God or being sent with the grim prediction that no one would listen to us. In a day when the realities of God's holy judgment on sin and of its eternal consequences are muted, those who are called and sent on any mission by the Lord need powerful reminders of these realities.

In contrast to this single use of send/go terminology in Isaiah 6, in Jeremiah 1 is a striking series of words. The Lord tells Jeremiah "I formed you," "I knew you," "I set you apart," and "I appointed you" (Jer. 1:5) From this point on, for Jeremiah's calling to be absolutely certain, it was necessary for God to perform specific acts of choosing.

While there are few people who are given anything like Jeremiah's assignment, most of us feel the need of some confirmation of our sending as well as our calling. We would appreciate the sights, sounds, and feelings described here. How God may speak to us today will be developed as we proceed.

God's people did not always listen to or obey the prophets he sent to them. "I sent you my servants the prophets. But they did not listen to me or pay attention" (Jer. 7:25). The Bible is also clear that there are false prophets who profess to speak for God, whom he has not sent. Jeremiah faced this problem. "The prophets are prophesying lies in my name. I have not sent them or appointed them or spoken to them ... I did not send them" (Jer. 14:14-15; see also Jer. 23:21, 32). Not only did God's true servants need to be sure of their commission; the people needed to discern which were genuine and which were false prophets.

Ezekiel's call and sending contain elements that are similar to that of Isaiah and Jeremiah in that the accomplishment of the task to which they were sent was going to be immensely difficult (Ezek. 2:1-8). Unique, of course, is the dramatic vision of creatures and wheels in chapter 1. While this passage is a hermeneutical challenge, the conclusion of the first chapter makes it all relevant. "This was the appearance of the likeness of the glory of the Lord. When I saw it, I fell facedown, and I heard the voice of one speaking" (v. 28). This leads into chapter 2. "He said to me ... I will speak to you ... I am sending you" (2:1-3). The person today who feels called by God may not have such a remarkable vision, but unless they are in devout, obedient fellowship with the Lord to sense his glorious presence and leading, the church might well question their sending.

Motivational missionary speakers often cite the experience of Jonah as someone who was sent ("Go," 1:2) but who disobeyed ("Jonah ran away from the Lord," 1:3). Let us look at this account of Jonah. God said, "Go to Nineveh and preach against it, because its wickedness has come up before me" (Jonah 1:2). Jonah's immediate response was to run away from the Lord for he knew what he was getting into. God didn't leave Jonah alone but followed him, even causing a mighty wind to threaten the boat he was on. He went before Jonah into the sea and prepared the large fish to swallow him. It was during the quiet time in the fish that Jonah began to reflect on how God had saved him when he cried out to him. The second time when God told Jonah, "Go," he obeyed.

Then came an interesting turn in Jonah's thinking and also God's. After he had proclaimed that God would destroy Nineveh if they did not repent, the people heard, believed God, and repented. God relented and did not bring on the destruction. Jonah, on the other hand, was angry and said that this was the reason he did not go to Nineveh in the first place, for he knew this would happen. He knew that God was gracious and compassionate. Later, God provided the gourd for Jonah's comfort from the heat of the sun, and when it died during the night, Jonah was angry again. In both cases, the incident of the saving of the people of Nineveh and the dying of the gourd, God asked Jonah, "Is it right for you to be angry?" Jonah replied, "It is." Jonah's concern was for the dying of the gourd, and God's concern was for the thousands of people who repented and were saved.

Can we include this incident as a negative response to God's call? Like Jonah, we know God's Word, but fear can often hinder our obedience to God's call. We want to respond to the need but are afraid of what God might require of us. To step out in faith not knowing the future, leaving family and friends, living in a new culture and primitive living conditions, all can play a part in our running away. While certainly not a model, Jonah's flight from the Lord and his petulance serve as both a negative example of one' response to God's calling and sending and as a reminder of God's sovereign grace and restoration.

The statistics regarding pastors and missionaries who have withdrawn from their ministries can be heavily discouraging to anyone who feels called to serve the Lord. As for those who have had that experience, the question must arise as to whether they were genuinely called and sent. It is not appropriate here to offer advice as to what steps should be taken in such cases or whether such individuals may biblically be restored to their ministries. What must be questioned is whether they were adequately prepared and whether their accrediting church or sending organization properly discerned their calling.

The last references to sending in the Old Testament are the famous predictions in Malachi 3:1 and 4:5. "I will send my messenger, who will prepare the way before me. Then suddenly the Lord you are seeking will come to his temple; the messenger of the covenant, whom you desire, will come, says the Lord Almighty." "See, I will send you the prophet Elijah before that great and dreadful day of the Lord comes." These two promises have been understood in different ways, but the first clearly refers to John the Baptist, as seen in Matthew 3:3. He was the one "sent by God" (John 1:6) to prepare the way for the Lord Jesus Christ, who himself was sent by God, which is a major theme in John and a truth we must recognize to have eternal life (John 5:24).

## New Testament

John the Baptist and the Lord Jesus thus join the company of those whom God called and sent. As we turn to the New Testament, we want to keep in mind that this great company does not disappear at the end of the Bible but continues today. To understand further what we might expect in the course of God calling and sending us into the world to represent him, we want to see more of what that involved in biblical times and how the Lord's servants received assurance as to their being called and sent.

Where should we begin? Actions of calling and sending occur throughout the New Testament. The first instance in the chronological order of New Testament books is in Matthew where we hear the familiar words of the Lord Jesus, "Ask the Lord of the harvest, therefore, to send out workers into his harvest field" (Matt. 9:38). Immediately after that, Matthew records that Jesus sent out the twelve apostles (10:5-8).

Turning to Mark, we see that Mark immediately connects his narrative with the prophecy at the end of the Old Testament that we have just considered, Malachi 3:1. He includes the word *send*, which is not in Matthew's shorter quotation concerning John the Baptist. Luke first uses that word in his narrative about Jesus' teaching at the synagogue at Nazareth. Jesus quotes Isaiah 61:1, 2, where sent is in parallel with anointed to describe the prophetic ministry Jesus applied to himself (Luke 4:18).

The first occurrences of sending are different in each of the Synoptic Gospels. In Matthew, it is the sending of disciples, in Mark the sending of John the Baptist, and in Luke the sending of Jesus himself. We will return to each of these gospels, but first it is important to observe that Mark, like John, employs the word *beginning* in the first verse of his gospel. "The beginning of the good news about Jesus the Messiah." John's beginning is more familiar to most people. "In the beginning was the Word." Both Mark and John remind us of Genesis 1:1. Therefore, a reader who is eager to get to the beginning of Jesus' ministry as described in Mark may not pause to grasp the significance of the other beginning in Mark, that of the preparatory ministry of John the Baptist. Mark offers the prophetic content of Malachi 3:1, coupled with Isaiah 40:3, as a description of that ministry. The words *I will send my messenger* therefore place God's action of sending at the very beginning of Mark's narrative and message. This is not a casual use of the word *send*. The whole gospel message in the Bible, and in biblical preaching across the centuries, is about God's act of sending the Lord Jesus Christ to be our Savior. This message and the messengers stand in continuity with God's actions not just across centuries but across millennia.

In his beginning section, Mark himself does not develop the theme of sending as John does. John does not quote Malachi on John the Baptist as Mark and Luke do. Shortly after opening with the famous Christological affirmation "In the beginning was the Word," John turns, abruptly, to the other messenger, John the Baptist. "There was a man sent from God whose name was John" (John 1:6). Just as abruptly after that introduction to John, the author returns to Christ, picking up the image of light in verse 5, "The light shines in darkness," with the statement "The true light that gives light to everyone was coming into the world" (v. 9). The alternation between Christ and John the Baptist then continues.

This is a powerful way John has of establishing the superiority of Christ over John the Baptist and, by extension, over all of the other prophets. After another strong affirmation concerning Christ in verse 14, "The Word became flesh," John again turns his attention to John the Baptist in verse 15. "John testified concerning him." After a further Christological statement in verses 16-18, there is a narrative dialogue in which John the Baptist refers to himself as the one who was sent to baptize (v. 33f). What we have observed here is the introduction of both Jesus and John the Baptist within this theme of sending. What he was sent to do is included in the message we are sent to proclaim.

We cannot proclaim clearly what we do not understand ourselves. It would not be sufficient for us simply to state the fact that there are many references in this gospel to the Father sending the Son. We need to experience the impact of these affirmations that come not only from the words in their individual contexts but in the cumulative force of their repetition. After his resurrection, Jesus said to his disciples, "As the Father has sent me, I am sending you" (John 20:21). This statement echoes words that are in Jesus' prayer just prior to his arrest and crucifixion. "As you sent me into the world, I have sent them into the world" (17:18). That the Greek could also be translated "just as" must not be overlooked or minimized. There is something about the *way* Jesus ministered that applies to us whom he has sent. There is also the unexpressed mandate that as we are sent, we must embody the reality at the core of the gospel that all Jesus did was in obedience to the Father who sent him. Our relationship to him in the sending/going process must replicate his relationship to the Father.

Some background is helpful here. Generation after generation had been taught, "Hear, Israel, the Lord our God, the Lord is one." The Jewish religion was an ethical monotheism and the Trinity was not a familiar concept. Therefore, they were not prepared to accept someone claiming to be God but would have considered such a claim to be arrogant blasphemy. Groundwork needed to be laid, and step by step, the witness Christ gave concerning himself, the witness provided by his works and the witness of God the Father, needed to be accepted. We see the development of this groundwork in the way the gospel of John presents Christ, and we will see also the connection between that and the mission on which Christ sends his disciples.

After reading John's soaring proclamation, "In the beginning was the Word," after the initial awareness of the first disciples as to Jesus' true identity, and after the dramatic conclusion to chapter 1 with the vision of "the angels of God ascending and descending on the Son of Man," we find ourselves enrolled, so to speak, in Christianity 101. In chapter 2 of John, Jesus changes the water into wine, a miracle that apparently only the disciples grasped, and he clears the temple, with the result that the onlookers demand some evidence of his authority. Chapter 3 describes the conversation between Jesus and Nicodemus, who assumed that Jesus was a teacher who came from God. That chapter ends with a final description of the ministry of John the Baptist during which we read that "the one whom God has sent speaks the words of God" (3:34). This is an important instance of the word "sent" being applied to Christ.

The next person to speak with Jesus after Nicodemus in John's narrative is the Samaritan woman who called him a prophet (4:19). She muses about the coming Messiah, and Jesus applies that term to himself (4:26). The narrative concludes with the people referring to him as the "Savior of the world" (4:42).

In chapter 5, the progressive unveiling of Jesus' identity is taken a step further when Jesus describes himself as the obedient Son of his heavenly Father. This revelation is itself part of a step-by-step progression: Jesus does the work of his Father, the Father loves the Son, the Son has the Father's authority to give life and to judge, and people should honor the Son just as they honor the Father who sent him (5:16-23). This progression of revelation continues in John through the numerous repeated occurrences of statements that Jesus was sent by the Father. The essence of Jesus' ministry, his food as he put it, was to "do the will of him who sent me" (John 4:34f), and he described the ministry of his disciples as being sent to reap a harvest described in terms of eternal life (4:35–38).

All this may seem to be unrelated to us being sent into the world of the twenty-first century, but consider this: in the gospel of John, the deity of Christ is progressively revealed as he fulfills his role as the one whom God the Father had sent. Jesus sought to win over the trust of people through his obedient Sonship to his Father, their God. Furthermore, the saving gospel that we like to proclaim through John 3:16 is described in the very next verse here (v. 17) in terms of Jesus being sent. The verb *send* in verse 17 is parallel to *gave* in verse 16. "For God so loved the world that he gave his one and only Son … For God did not send his son into the world to condemn the world but to save the world through him." Thus the very gospel we are sent to proclaim incorporates the fact of his being *sent*.

To get the force of this, consider these passages in sequence:

> "He who does not honor the Son does not honor the Father, who sent him. (5:23).

> "I seek not to please myself but him who sent me" (5:30).

> "The very work that the Father has given me to finish, and which I am doing, testify that the Father has sent me" (5:36).

"The Father who sent me has himself testified concerning me" (5:37).

"And this is the will of him who sent me" (6:39).

"For I have come down from heaven not do my will but to do the will of him who sent me" (6:38).

"No one can come to me unless the Father who sent me draws him, and I will raise him up at the last day" (6:44).

"Just as the living Father sent me…" (6:57).

"My teaching is not my own. It comes from him who sent me" (7:16).

"I am not here on my own, but he who sent me is true" (7:28).

"I know him because I am from him and he sent me" (7:29).

"I am with you for only a short time, and then I go to the one who sent me" (7:33).

"If I do judge, my decisions are right, because I am not alone. I stand with the Father, who sent me" (8:16).

"I am one who testifies for myself; my other witness is the father, who sent me" (8:18).

"He who sent me is reliable, and what I have heard from him I tell the world" (8:26).

"The one who sent me is with me; he has not left me alone, for I always do what pleases him" (8:29).

"If God were your Father, you would love me, for I came from God and now am here. I have not come on my own; but he sent me" (8:42).

"As long as it is day, we must do the work of him who sent me" (9:4).

"What about the one whom the Father set apart as his very own and sent into the world?" (10:36).

"[Father,] I said this for the benefit of the people standing here, that they may believe that you sent me" (11:42).

"When a person believes in me, he does not believe in me only, but in the one who sent me" (12:44).

"When he looks at me, he sees the one
who sent me" (12:45).

The cumulative force of these quotations is to identify
closely the Father and the Son he sent. This is important
*theologically* regarding the relationship of the three persons
within the Trinity. It is also significant *evangelistically*
regarding the content of the gospel message. In addition,
it is a substantial *foundation* for the ministry of those who
are sent today in the name of Christ, a major subject in
his thoughts during the closing days of his earthly life.
When he washed his disciples' feet, he told them to do
this for each other, saying "No servant is greater than
his master, nor is a messenger greater than the one who
sent him" (John 13:16). He told his disciples, "Whoever
accepts anyone I send accepts me; and whoever accepts
me accepts the one who sent me" (13:20).

In contrast, those who persecuted Jesus would
persecute his disciples because they did not know the
one who sent him (John 15:20-21). In his prayer recorded
in John 17, Jesus first prays concerning himself and his
mission, saying that eternal life consisted in knowing God
and the one God had sent (v. 3). Then he prays for his
disciples, who believed that the Father had sent him (vv.
8, 25). It is in this context that Jesus said, "As you sent me
into the world, I have sent them into the world" (v. 18).
Furthermore, their unity in the Lord was to be a means of
the world believing that God had sent Christ (vv. 21-23).

The significance of all this must not be missed. Jesus
has made extensive sayings about his being sent by the
Father. Now he makes the statement that he is sending

his disciples in the same way that he was sent, and he does this in his crucial, sacred prayer of consecration. This is astonishing. It places the Christian ministry and mission in the brilliant, intense, eternal light of the Holy Trinity. The one who said to his Father, "Here I am ... I have come to do your will, my God" (Heb. 10:17) and who was "obedient to death—even death on a cross" (Phil. 2:8) now says to his Father that he is sending his servants in the same way.

There is more. After his resurrection, Jesus said directly to his disciples, "Peace be with you! As the Father has sent me, I am sending you" (John 20:21). Now Jesus tells them what he has already said to the Father in his prayer. All the weight of this truth, that the Father sent the Son, is now placed on the disciples and their mission. This is no mere sentiment.

Now we are ready to understand that to be sent *as* the Son was sent by the Father means far more than being a Christian worker, a messenger, a preacher, a missionary. It means that we are to have a relationship with Christ like he had with his Father. It means complete obedience to our Lord. It means living and working in unity with other disciples and with Christ, just as he worked in complete unity with the Father. It means testifying to the relationship of the Son to the Father. It means proclaiming the gospel of the one whom God gave out of love for the world and whom God sent into that world not to condemn but to save it. Are those who believe that they are called by God and who want to be sent into the world in his name aware of what it means to be sent by Christ just as the Father sent him? Do churches that ordain or otherwise commission people to serve God in various ministries take all the implication of the Father sending the Son into consideration when they make their decisions regarding whom to send? If, as we have seen, the Jewish concept of sending a representative was that such a person was to be accepted as the person who sent them, think of the implications when we are sent by the one who was sent by the Father!

With that context of John in mind, we can meaningfully return and review examples of sending in the other gospels. The first instance of sending terminology in the canonical order of the New Testament is in the famous saying of Jesus, "Ask the Lord of the harvest, therefore, to send out workers into his harvest field" (Matt. 9:38). Immediately after that, Matthew records that Jesus sent out the twelve apostles (10:5-8). Their mission was to proclaim that "the kingdom of heaven has come near," and Jesus added a warning. "I am sending you out like sheep among wolves" (v. 16).

This sending has parallels in Mark 3:13-15, in which, as we saw earlier, Mark uses the word *called* (and in Luke 9:1-6). Luke also describes the sending of a larger group (10:1-12). Without going into details, it is useful to note that in all three gospels, the disciples' missions included healing, and in all three gospels (except in regard to that larger group), it included the casting out of demons. Matthew alone mentions raising the dead among their duties. Also, each of these sending narratives, except Mark, refers to the kingdom. The fact that one or another of these missions includes such substantial activities as announcing the kingdom, healing, and casting out of demons emphasizes the importance of the sending. The sober aspect of this is that those whom God sends, beginning with the Old Testament prophets, are persecuted and even killed (Luke 11:49). That fact is pictured also in one of Jesus parables, which Luke relates in 20:16, about the vineyard.

Choosing on God's part should issue in our discernment of the will of God. His calling and his sending should issue in action on the part of the church. The church appoints *(designates* or perhaps *ordains)* individuals and sends them out with whatever financial support is appropriate.

These are simple statements. There should be a confluence of actions that involve God, the church, and the individual. Too often, Christians who feel called are stranded, feeling isolated, sometimes going from church to church trying to get support. Meanwhile, their church should have been proactive, praying God to send workers (Matt. 9:38) and praying for discernment as to whom in the church God has chosen for them to send.

# 5

# The Local Church: The Bridge

There is a bridge in Milwaukee, Wisconsin, called the Hoan Bridge. It is near Lake Michigan, starting in downtown Milwaukee. It has also been called "the bridge to nowhere," a fine-looking structure with a 1,140-foot steel arch. Although construction on the bridge began in 1970, it did not connect to any of the surrounding highway systems on the other end until 1998 when the long-proposed Lake Parkway extension from downtown Milwaukee to Mitchell Airport was completed. Today, the bridge is known for its beautiful views of the city and Lake Michigan. Most citizens today acknowledge that the bridge takes them somewhere important, rather than nowhere.

Perhaps you know someone who feels that their life is like that bridge. Someone who feels called to Christian service but who has not found a destination or a means (perhaps a church) to help fulfill that calling. Is that person you? Or are you a church leader who knows someone like that? Perhaps you are a pastor who earnestly wishes that someone in your church would show evidence of being called, so that you could work with them to accomplish

God's will in their life. Maybe you are the chair of a church missions committee who hopes that among the many people requesting financial support would be someone who is seeking mainly guidance and encouragement from the committee.

On the other hand, you may be a missionary candidate who has been traveling from church to church seeking support, wishing that there was a better way to be sent out than having to compete in a crowded field for limited funds. Are you the executive of a missionary organization, who is sensitive to the burden of under-supported missionaries? Do you know of many eager potential candidates who were converted at university and do not have a supporting church? And how about you who pastor a university community church? It has become the major spiritual home of many students. As their numbers grow year after year, are they more than you can help sponsor as they go on to seminary or directly into missions or some other ministry?

How do we complete the bridge? How can we help those whom God seems to be calling? How can we help those who need someone to discern whether they are indeed called, and if so, affirm them and perhaps send them? How can we proactively seek potential servants of God, whose calling goes beyond the marketplace, at the same time that we encourage those whose field *is* the marketplace? How can we help mission agencies by assuming more of the responsibilities that churches should have in partnership with those agencies?

It takes much time, many workers, and extensive means to complete the bridge of each life from conversion to service for the Master Builder. We can be grateful that the architectural plans, though perhaps neglected, have not been lost. We need to grasp the expansive perspective of Paul's letter to the Ephesians in order to understand the larger aspect of calling.

After Paul breaks through the world that ignores the Gentiles, showing that God's mystery embraces their inclusion in the church, he opens a vista that we would never see except by revelation. The word *mystery* in the biblical writings refers to God's purposes and plans that are gradually unfolded by revelation at successive stages of history. Paul is ready to unveil the new vista in Ephesians 3:10, 11. "His intent was that now, through the church, the manifold wisdom of God should be made known to the rulers and authorities in the heavenly realms, according to his eternal purpose that he accomplished in Christ Jesus our Lord."

It is abundantly clear in Scripture that there are beings—both good and evil—in the universe beyond our little planet. The church not only exists to win converts and rescue them from eternal condemnation for their own benefit; it also exists to bring glory to the Creator of the universe and the Savior of the church. Worship is not a sidebar. When members of a church sit down to write (or rewrite) a statement of mission, they will likely list local and world evangelism as the church's main objective. But the reason for the church's existence—that is, its ultimate purpose—transcends even its important mission of evangelism.

Paul gives us a clue regarding this purpose in a passage that can easily be overlooked: Romans 15:16. "He gave me the priestly duty of proclaiming the Gospel of God, so that the Gentiles might be an offering acceptable to God, sanctified by the Holy Spirit." Using what we might call Old Testament sacrificial language, Paul graphically describes himself as a priest who approaches God's heavenly temple and presents Gentile converts to God for his glory. The reason, ultimately, that any of us, Jew or Gentile, is rescued from judgment is that we might bring glory to God. That is also the reason for the existence of the church.

We have seen that, according to 1 Corinthians 1:18, 19, "the message of the cross is foolishness" to unbelievers, but "to us who are being saved," it is "the power of God and the wisdom of God" (1:24). A major problem in the church at Corinth was that God's wisdom was being obscured by the lack of unity among the believers. The unity of believers demonstrates the effectiveness of the saving and reconciling work of Christ and the wisdom of God in his divine plan of salvation. Therefore, to understand the teaching that it is "through the church" that the "rulers and authorities in the heavenly realms" recognize "the manifold wisdom of God" (Eph. 3:10), both the preceding and the following contexts must be taken into consideration. The preceding context (3:2-9) reveals the mystery of God in uniting Jew and Gentile in the church through the gospel, and the following context hammers home the truth of the oneness of believers in the church, the "one body" that knows the love of Christ (3:14–4:6). Paul's prayer summarizes all this, which is "immeasurably more than all we ask or imagine" (3:20) by declaring "to him be glory in the church and in Christ Jesus throughout all generations for ever and ever!" (3:21). Of course, we expect God to receive glory through Christ, but here is a remarkable statement that it is also through the church, which by its unity displays the wisdom of God.

## What Does the Church Have to Do with the Call?

First of all, the church itself has been called to display God's wisdom, both in the neighborhood of the local church and to beings "in the heavenly realms" of this immense universe. Second, individuals in the church have been specifically called to help maintain the unity that brings honor to God. When Paul appeals to the whole church to "make every effort to keep the unity of the spirit of the bond of peace" (4:3), he explains that every believer has been given God's grace, clearly meaning not only saving grace but grace to serve. He quotes from Psalm 68:18. "When he ascended on high he took many captives and gave gifts to his people."

The language in that verse of the psalm recalls that of Numbers 18:6, which says that the Levites were a gift to Aaron. Numbers 8:14 says that the Levites were set apart from the other people of Israel. This was signified when the Israelites laid their hands on the Levites (8:10). As we have seen in the experience of Joshua (Num. 27:22, 23), the laying on of hands can be a public indication of the appointment of someone, and in a different context, the same thing is true regarding the sending of Saul and Barnabas in Acts 13:3.

So far, we have seen that the church itself has been called to demonstrate by its unity the wisdom of God. That is its primary calling. Second, all individuals in the church have received gifts apportioned by God. This indicates their calling. The first aspect of the church's calling involves, as we have seen, cosmic dimension that is defined in terms of the "heavenly realms" (Eph. 3:10-11). The second is linked to the ascension of Christ, he who "fills the whole universe" (4:10). But now a third phase, with a new aspect of calling, appears and also is linked to our Lord's ascension. Given its heavenly orientation, it is of immense importance—far greater than might be expected if viewed in isolation from the context of 3:2-4:10.

The transition from gifts being given to individuals to individuals being given to the church, with both being linked to Psalm 68, is remarkable. This passage is of immense significance when we ask the question of whether there are some people who are called to ministry in a sense that others are not. The answer has to be in accordance with the flow of this whole passage. All are called, all are gifted spiritually, but some are given back to the church for special ministries. It is not that some are called and others are not. It is not that some are called to secular vocations and others to religious vocations (with 1 Cor. 7, especially vs. 17-24 as a proof passage). Rather, in the context of secular society, all are called to legitimate vocations, and in the context of the church, all are called to spiritual ministries. In those realms, there is no clergy-laity distinction. All believers are priests. After centuries of separation between clergy and laity, the latter decades of the twentieth century saw an emphasis on the ministry of the laity, and in many quarters, there is a tendency to obliterate any difference between laity and clergy. The superb book on calling by Os Guinness, *The Call,* has helped many to see that they have a calling as legitimate as do those in religious service. But Ephesians teaches us that in terms of building the church (through evangelism) and of bringing unity and maturity to the church (through preaching, teaching and caring), there are some who have a special function, a special ministry, and we would say a special calling.

I once wrote an article in connection with a question about ministry in which I suggested doing reverse contextualization. We often take it for granted that the structure of the church, its manner of worship, and its ministries today are the same as in New Testament times. Therefore, we answer questions about ministry from that standpoint. We talk about contextualizing the gospel for foreign cultures. We would do the same for forms of ministry. But what about bringing our forms of ministry to the profiles of the New Testament church and seeing if they fit? With regard to calling, we may require a pastor to be called, but what about the Sunday school superintendent? Certainly, teachers were among the choice group of those whom God gave to the church to equip believers for ministry (Eph. 4:7-16). Should we expect a calling (or require ordination) for those who teach in a particular venue but not in others? Should elders be called and ordained? Some churches answer positively. And further, did the early church listen to the same preacher all, or even most, Sundays, or was there interaction and mutual ministry? A look at 1 Corinthians 14 suggests the latter.

To discuss all this is not to say that the structures cannot change, or that we should not have pastors and preachers, but rather that we must not fit square pegs into round holes. There are many terms that express our relationship to Jesus our Lord. They are significant terms in the gospels, where the disciples actually traveled with Jesus and expressed their obedience in concrete ways at his command. They are all aspects of our response to the call of the Lord Jesus, which is the call of God.

# The Church's Response to God's Call

The biblical evidence points to a distinct call to church ministry and missions, that is, to special service to God both within an established church and beyond (whether called evangelism, church planting, or missions in general). The reasons for this include the following:

1. Obedience to biblical instructions and adherence to models that are clearly intended to be norms
2. The importance of having people clearly able, prepared, and spiritually qualified to lead the church and represent the Lord in the world
3. The personal demands (mental, spiritual, and physical) of special ministries and especially of cross cultural missions
4. The drastic changes in one's lifestyle, material circumstances, possessions, and family relationships that may be required

The value of and spiritual investment in, say, being a pastor in an overseas church may be no greater than teaching a home Bible class one day a week, but the demands and requirements are certainly different.

It is not that one form is ministry and another not. Rather, it is that the consequences of ineptness, failure, or spiritual collapse are magnified in the case of a church leader or missionary. Those who serve and represent the church ought to be sure of their calling, and so should the church. It has become common for the calling of all believers to be emphasized (as it should be) on the one hand, but on the other hand, the elevation to prominence of people who have strong personal traits and ministries to push the ministry of called, committed, and spiritually anointed servants of the Lord into the shadows.

Yet there is another extreme circumstance that needs to be avoided. That is the exclusion of the so-called laity from recognition and opportunity. The Bible knows no distinction between clergy and laity, even though it does display a difference between those whose calling is in the marketplace and those whose calling is to give up life in the marketplace in order to concentrate on special ministries, depending on God to provide their daily support. It seems to be a human failure that we cannot give equal acknowledgement and attention to different callings of God without elevating one above the other. The Reformation emphasis on the priesthood of all believers went only so far. The ecclesiastical position of a few kept the priesthood from the many. Even the recovery of the ministry of the laity in the latter twentieth century failed in most quarters. Did they allow ordinary believers to baptize persons they brought to Christ? Did they allow women to collect the offering, to serve communion, or more? A very important question comes into play again at this point. Given what we know about God's call and the work of the Holy Spirit in the church, should we be really be talking about a special call? After all, with the priesthood of all believers, and the gifting of all Christians by the Holy Spirit, is it not elitist to think about a special call that only some receive while others do not?

The priesthood of all believers has to be understood against the background of priesthood in the Old Testament. That designation was limited to descendents of Levi through Aaron, who represented the people by offering sacrifices to the Lord. The rest of Levi's descendents, who were called Levites, served in a supportive role to the priests, with various responsibilities related to the temple and worship. When Christ offered his life sacrificially for us on the cross, he became both the sacrifice and our great high priest. (The whole book of Hebrews relates to this, especially 7:26-28 and chapters 8 and 9.) It was not necessary, therefore, for the Christian church to continue either the sacrifices or a priesthood to offer them. There did, however, remain an aspect of priesthood that was not restricted to a particular order. Peter refers to Christians as "a royal priesthood" (1 Peter 2:9). This clearly refers to all the people of God, believers who are no longer alienated by sin and no longer dependent on a special class of priests to approach God on their behalf. They are a people who are in a new position of nearness to God. They have a special place in the kingdom of God and constitute a royal priesthood. In the Old Testament and until a radical change during the period of the Maccabees, priests and kings belonged to separate lineages that did not overlap. This is a further step.

We need to see how this new identity, which is true of all believers, differs from the identity of those whom Ephesians describes as God's gifts to the people of God (Eph. 4:8, which is a rewording and new application of Psalm 68:18). It would seem logical to conclude that if some are the Lord's special gifts to the people of God, that special group is not coextensive with the whole people of God. Furthermore, when Ephesians 4:11 names those whom Christ gave to his church—"the apostles, the prophets, the evangelists, the pastors and teachers"—their function is "to equip his people for works of service." All the people do "works of service," and they need to be equipped to do this. There is a distinction between the individuals who have special ministries, who constitute God's gifts to his people and who *do* the equipping of the people, on the one hand, and, on the other hand, the whole people of God who constitute the royal priesthood and who are the saints who are *being* equipped.

There seems also to be a distinction in Romans 12 between these personal gifts to the church and the various members of the body who perform various needed functions in the church. We might say that some of those functions seem to be categorized into identifiable servants of the Lord. The latter not only, for example, do teaching but are teachers. They have special ministries of teaching in the church. All God's people *have* gifts, and all *are* gifts. See also 1 Corinthians 12 and the distinction between all members of the body in verses 12-26 and those special servants God has "placed in the church" and done so in a designated order (vv. 27-31).

Let us keep in mind the possible meanings of ministry. The short answer is that it simply means service. But a longer answer is that it means different things in the Bible and describes different kinds of service. The word *kind* used in the NIV, for example, translates different Greek and Hebrew words, and three times, there is no corresponding word in the Greek text; it is part of an expanded English phrase. We might close this section with several reminders.

Abilities do not prove a calling. Many capable people are not called. Conversely, a lack of abilities does not disprove a calling. Nevertheless, the probability of calling to a difficult ministry is lower if one lacks relevant abilities. However, one's feelings of inadequacy are not proof that one is not called. The assessment and wisdom of one's church leaders is of major importance, though not infallible proof of either calling or noncalling.

# The Calling of Elders and Deacons

Here we want to look at the questions of whether serving as an elder or deacon requires a special calling from God, and if so, how that calling is discerned.

Regarding elders, a brief look at their purpose and qualifications will help as we consider these questions. Jewish Christians in the first century were familiar with elders from their own synagogues. It was, however, necessary for Paul to instruct the elders in the church at Ephesus as to the purpose for their existence in that church (Acts 20:28-31). The important words are *keep watch* and *be shepherds*. Peter's words in the 1 Peter 5:2-4 agree with this. "Be shepherds of God's flock that is under your care, watching over them, not because you must, but because you are willing, as God wants you to be." The elders are "not pursuing dishonest gain, but eager to serve; not lording it over those entrusted to you, but being examples to the flock." Then in 1 Timothy 3 and in Titus 1, the contexts make it clear that the elders are expected to guard the flock from false teaching. This responsibility certainly calls for elders who are doctrinally perceptive. The importance of the teaching role of elders is seen in 1 Timothy 5:17. "The elders who direct the affairs of the church well are worthy of double honor, especially those whose work is preaching and teaching."

If that is the case, are the elders the same people as those described in Ephesians 4:11-13 as pastors and teachers? And if this comprehensive term (the Greek structure links the two words implying that they refer to the same people) can be understood to describe the basic ministry of the typical church pastor today, do we have grounds for thinking that there is at least an overlap between elders and pastors? In some denominations, pastors are considered elders. It would seem then that our discussion about calling could well apply to elders as well as to pastors. Biblically, elders are indeed pastors and shepherds of the flock.

The instructions also make it clear that beyond the qualification of doctrinal knowledge, the dominant qualifications for eldership and the diaconate are moral. In none of the relevant passages, however, are there specific instructions as to how the elders and deacons are to be chosen, or from our perspective, how they are called. On the one hand, it is certainly true that the congregations should be able to recognize those who are qualified to be elders and deacons without necessarily going through the process of a vote or of some other selective process. On the other hand, we need to ask how those whom God wants to be elders or deacons know this. They should have as clear a sense of being called as did Paul, Timothy, and Titus. And who makes the decision as to which persons out of a pool of potential candidates are truly called? In Acts 14:23, Paul and Barnabas "appointed elders for them in each church and, with prayer and fasting, committed them to the Lord, in whom they had put their trust." It is clear that Paul and Barnabas used sound judgment as to which of the men had demonstrated spiritual growth sufficient to warrant choosing them. Little is said beyond this. Elsewhere, we must assume that individuals were similarly recognized as being spiritually mature.

Another question relates to the larger issue of whether a special call is needed for a short or limited term of service or for a lifetime ministry. The application of this to elders (focusing on them for now) depends on whether one considers their appointment to be lifetime or not. Logically there are just three possibilities. First, once appointed, a person is an elder for life and serves actively and continuously as such. Second, once appointed, a person is an elder for life but serves actively only when asked for specific terms, which are not necessarily continuous. And finally, the appointment is initially only for a limited term of service, though it may be renewable. For our purposes here, it is perhaps appropriate to say that whether for short, long or lifetime appointment, any individual who serves as an elder should have the qualifications discussed here. Put negatively, no one who lacks these qualifications could be called by God.

As to the actual calling of elders, we should begin with Acts 14:23. "Paul and Barnabas appointed elders for them in each church and, with prayer and fasting, committed them to the Lord, in whom they had put their trust." The setting of this action was a circle of churches that comprised people who had only recently become believers through the ministry of Paul and Barnabas. No doubt, most of them were Jewish and therefore had some understanding of the role of elders. Perhaps some were God-fearers—Gentiles who believed in the God of the Old Testament, embraced Jewish morals, and attended the synagogue. They too would have had some understanding of what it meant to be an elder. But these churches would have needed some instruction by Paul and Barnabas about the work of Christian elders. Those who were to be appointed as elders needed assurance that God had called them. The churches needed instruction as to how to recognize such leaders.

The book of Acts does not directly answer such questions here, but it does have an example of another group who were chosen for a different purpose, and in the narrative in Acts 6, we have a clue as to the process of qualification and selection. Acts describes the situation in the early church when a minority group (whose culture was derived from the Greek culture, and whose language reflected this) felt that their widows were being neglected by Jews. Their culture and language were, of course, Semitic. The twelve apostles recognized that micromanagement was not appropriate for them and that they needed to concentrate on the ministry of God's Word. Their solution was for the church to take responsibility to find those who were "full of the Spirit and wisdom" and to select people from among them to care for the daily food distribution. It is common to assume that these were the first deacons. Perhaps this was so in a rudimentary way, although they were not so named here. But more importantly from this narrative, we learn how the early church was taught to take responsibility for their own organization and to value character and spirituality in those who appeared qualified to serve.

Although the narratives of the book of Acts are descriptive and not all of them necessarily paradigmatic, in chapter 6 we do learn the importance of spiritual and moral character even in people appointed to "wait on tables" (Acts 6:2-4). This accords with what we have observed in 1 Timothy and in Titus about the character of elders and deacons. The role of Paul in appointing elders may or may not point the way to apostolic succession, but it certainly shows that elders are not self-appointed. Also in that case, at least the initial group of elders was chosen by a missionary/evangelist, Paul, who led them to Christ and founded the church.

Paul's role in those instances, and also the role of the church acting under the directions of the apostles in selecting those who served in Acts 6, can be compared with the role of Timothy and Titus and their churches in selecting elders and deacons. According to those epistles, the churches were to follow the directions of Timothy and Titus who, in turn, were following the instructions of Paul. This provides a precedent for the church and its leaders taking initiative in selecting others for positions of leadership. There seems to be no precedent, however, of any person acting individually and independently claiming that they are following a true calling of God and therefore taking authority to themselves in the church. (This calls to mind 1 Tim. 2:11-12, where Paul's use of an unusual Greek verb [*authentein*] hints at an unwarranted assumption of individual authority by women.) If further evidence is needed, we can recall that even the great apostle Paul needed someone else, Ananias, to find him and to have a part in the restoration of his vision and his commissioning by the Lord. All this seems to indicate a pattern of the way God called his servants in the New Testament church: *through existing leadership.*

This is by no means the end of the story. In 1 Timothy 3:1, Paul wrote, "Whoever aspires to be an overseer desires a noble task." Does this contradict what we have just said against the individual assumption of leadership? By the time the letters to Timothy and Titus were written, there were many churches and many elders and deacons. Some supplementary instructions were needed concerning church life as well as regarding doctrine. No doubt, there were enough cases of people wanting to be elders that questions arose as to how to know which ones were truly called by God. So Paul begins by affirming that it is good for people to have humble aspirations to leadership and service. But it is also possible for people to have aspirations that arise from a desire for prominence and control. The way Paul proceeds to list the qualifications for eldership, and for the diaconate and their wives, implies that an aspiration does not in itself constitute a calling. Verification of such a calling is dependent on the church's recognition of a person's qualifications, both spiritually and morally.

# What Qualifications Were Important for the Church?

We are now at one of several tipping points in the process from calling to sending. A person may have a sincere desire to serve the Lord, a compassion for people who are in need, and a belief that God is calling them. Opportunities may lie ahead. A church may be eager to send people out in various ministries. Funding may be available. But is this person qualified to perform the ministry in view? Is such a person qualified today?

The key question, of course, is what do we mean by qualified in this context? We do not mean merely human expertise. The apostle Paul would rise up and shout, "No!" to that. After all, he made a huge point at the beginning of his first letter to the Corinthians about God using people who do not excel by human standards. God is glorified when spiritual accomplishments are attributed directly to him.

The fact is that Paul himself was highly qualified in this respect. The specific point of reference in 1 Corinthians was oratorical ability. This was highly regarded during the

Greco Roman period. Sophists were praised (sometimes with tongue in cheek) for "making a worse argument better and the better argument seem worse." Contrariwise, skilled speakers sometimes demeaned their own oratorical ability in order to make it seem that they were able to rise above their own limitations. This could have the result that their argument became even more effective. When Paul referred to his own limitations, however, he did not do that for the sake of some oratorical effect but because he recognized his own humanity and wanted the glory to go to the Lord.

All of this is important for our discussion of qualifications. We need not downplay God-given abilities to make sure that personal humility is honest and not an act. Lives are changed by the gospel through the power of the Holy Spirit. All this is of immense importance in both the Old Testament and New Testament about God's choice of leaders like David over others who demonstrated qualities of strength and leadership. We need therefore to consider spiritual obedience and maturity, spiritual gifting and serving, and fitting the qualifications to the need.

**Spiritual Obedience and Maturity:** There has been a strong emphasis in recent years on spiritual growth (or spiritual formation). It may be useful here to distinguish between being mature and being obedient, as it is possible, even though not usual, for a person to be one but not the other. Just as a child might be obedient to his parents faithfully but, for one reason or another, lag in his growth into mature adulthood, so a Christian could conceivably obey the Lord Jesus and the teachings of Scripture but never grow sufficiently to teach others. Usually, of course, such a condition indicates a lack of obedience. Conversely, a Christian can mature considerably in biblical and theological knowledge but be inconsistent in obedience and discipleship. Usually, those who are deficient in obedience do not mature and those who are mature are not disobedient, but the point is that it is possible for someone who feels called to some special ministry to be deficient in either obedience or maturity and therefore not qualified for that ministry.

Can the vitality of one's spiritual life be measured? To an extent, it can, but that involves the tricky matter of discerning motives. A person may conceivably want to become a missionary for the purpose of teaching the truth or of establishing a new outpost of their denomination without first of all being motivated by the love of Christ. Loving God with entire heart, soul, mind, and strength and loving our neighbors as ourselves should be an essential motive. Conversely, one may desire to help disadvantaged persons without doing so in order to present people as an offering to God for his glory. Motives, spiritual life, maturity, and obedience are crucial whether a church is thinking of calling and of sending someone as a missionary overseas or as a teaching elder in the church. Too often, other considerations take precedence, especially in the case of eldership, such as leadership ability, business acumen, or successful committee performance within the church. They also go beyond quantifiable measurements, such as whether the person has a daily quiet time of Bible reading and prayer. Among other quantifiable qualifications that are important, but insufficient, are education and success in prior ministry.

A neglected word in all of this is character. We must sadly admit that an occasional news headline about the unfaithfulness of a pastor or evangelist not only reflects on all of us but also portrays the carnality, the flesh that lurks within all of us. It is a fact that anyone can fall, but a long obedience and continual spiritual maturation strengthen us against that possibility. Usually, those who desire to be commissioned for, and supported in, specific ministries are relatively young and therefore, while eager to obey, are less likely to have a long record of maturity and faithfulness. Here, again, discernment is needed.

**Spiritual Gifting and Serving:** If all this is true, what kind of qualifications and abilities are we looking for? Basic capabilities need not detract from the glory of God! After all, they are God given. Common sense tells us that a lack of linguistic ability can be a serious detriment to someone who needs to learn a difficult language in another culture. How well one can work with others in a team ministry can be determined with some success through the use of one of several testing programs now available.

We would surely all agree that the main focus should be on spiritual gifts and spirituality. Both of those terms call for careful definition. First, the amount of attention given to spiritual gifts in 1 Corinthians 12 and in Romans 12 (without the unnecessary extra term *spiritual*) speaks for itself. It would be downright foolish to think that God is calling and that the church should send anyone who does not give evidence of spiritual gifts. But while these gifts can certainly be identified and organized in the biblical texts, to identify them in human beings is something else.

Before pursuing this further, let's ask what the phrase *spiritual gifts* means. Careful observation of 1 Corinthians 12, Romans 12, Ephesians 4, and 1 Peter 4 reveals a rather surprising assortment of terminology. *Gifts* refers to abilities, but also sometimes to the people who have these abilities. That is notably the case in Ephesians 4, but it is also true in 1 Corinthians 12:28-31. There are nouns and there are (especially in Greek) participles describing actions, phrases, and single words, the selected gifts, and the order they are in. This differs from passage to passage. Some interpreters think that the order is important; others do not.

Two other observations are crucial. One is that the lists contain both what we might call spiritual endowments and also what we normally refer to as natural abilities. Should we, therefore, distinguish between these? We might say that to work miracles, to speak in and interpret tongues, and to distinguish spirits are in no way the result of natural abilities, passed on genetically. Rather, the Spirit of God can give these gifts at any time, such as in a church gathering, as may be needed. In contrast, teaching and leadership are abilities that an individual has from birth and also perhaps training (nature and nurture). They do not exist just for one time.

Granting these differences, it is true of both types that they are God's gifts whether through our genes or bestowed on the spot. The introduction to chapter 12 in 1 Corinthians uses the Greek work *pneumatikon*, "spiritual, a spiritual matter," to describe the topics he is about to discuss. This is an apparent answer to one or more questions from the people in the Corinthian church. Although their question probably stems from the tendency of at least some Christians at Corinth to apply promises concerning future blessings and spiritual state to their present life on earth, Paul includes what we would call natural gifts in his discussion. Furthermore, in 1 Peter 4:10, each of the two gifts mentioned there are called just that, a gift (Greek *charisma*) that the recipients are to use "to serve others, faithfully administering God's grace in its various forms." The natural gifts that are transmitted genetically are, therefore, as much gifts of God's grace as they are to the unique spiritual endowments.

There are some curious discussions that people have about spiritual gifts. One is that the some gifts seem to be popular. We noticed earlier that many seminary students claim their gift is teaching. Perhaps a realistic assessment is that they naturally appreciate the ministry their professors have and want to do that. A different circumstance is that one might hear a couple (or a single person) say they have the gift of hospitality, so they give lavish parties. Basic care for travelers was essential in the days of the early church because of the difficulties of travel. But while hospitality is a commendable (and commanded) act of Christian love, it is not in the list of spiritual gifts. Those that are listed in 1 Corinthians 12:28 are clear and in some order of importance. "And in the church God has appointed first of all apostles, second prophets, third teachers, then workers of miracles, also those having gifts of healing, those able to help others, those with gifts of administration, and those speaking in different kinds of tongues."

In 1 Peter 4:8–10, the wording is different. "Above all, love each other deeply, because love covers over a multitude of sins. Offer hospitality to one another without grumbling. Each one should use whatever gift he has received to serve others, faithfully administering God's grace in its various forms." Further instructions relate to "speaking the very words of God." As for Ephesians, we might say that much of the whole book is summed up in the words derived from Psalm 68:18. "When he ascended on high, he led captives in his train and gave gifts to men" (Ephesians 4:8).

Rather than analyzing all these verses, we might make several relevant observations. One is that God's call assigns an extraordinary variety of tasks to Christians. Specific assignments usually include several of these tasks, but perhaps just one. Recently, a friend wrote me that she had observed that people in the area she was serving would take a survey or go to a retreat to find their gift. But the biblical way would be to realize that God gives gifts to the church—to an individual, yes, but for the service of God through the church—and one's gift is made visible as one is already in action, so to speak, in the church or elsewhere. In other words, people have to see something in order to affirm it as a gift. The assumption that one's gift has to appear before one serves is false.

We can now draw several conclusions about spiritual gifting and offer some suggestions: Every believer has some special gifts(s) from God. These are grace-gifts, for which we are indebted to God. Such a gift is ours only in the sense that it is ours to use. These gifts are not for our private use, for our own benefit, but "to serve others" (1 Peter 4:10) "for the common good" (1 Cor. 12:7). Since all believers are gifted, possession of a gift is, in itself, not evidence of a divine call to special service. The important question is whether a person is lovingly employing their gift(s) in service for the good of others.

**Fitting the Qualifications to the Need:** Through careful researching, church leaders should determine how pressing the need is for specially gifted individuals in a particular ministry. There are skills that may be common in one's secular work in this country but which are needed more seriously somewhere overseas. As such opportunities develop today, they may be more valuable than formerly, such as teaching English as a second language in a closed country. The circumstances presented as needs at missionary conferences today may offer just the right way to enter a country that otherwise would be closed.

In the introduction, I wrote of Pete Fleming's call to the jungles of Ecuador. The elders of his church had no difficulty seeing his qualifications filling the need in the secular university, but they had a problem with him using his abilities among the jungle Indians whose language was not even in writing. They finally did commend him to the work in Ecuador, not realizing that having a master's degree would have enabled him to get a passport into the country as a teacher. At that time, the country was closed to missionaries. The only way Olive was able to get in was for Pete to come home to marry her and have her on his passport. After Pete had been in the country a few years, some of the senior missionaries saw the value of his secular university's master's degree in American literature as a possible means of ministry in the university in Quito. Even some of the Christian students came to Pete and Olive's house to ask him questions and even pleaded with him to be involved with the university students. They were facing teaching that Pete could help them with because of his own secular university training. He considered this possible ministry for the future but believed that God's specific call at that time was to the work in the jungles. It was not until after the five men were killed and their deaths were widely known that the country opened up to missionaries. It was also their sacrifice that alerted people worldwide to the ongoing needs of unreached tribes and motivated many to volunteer. What had appeared to be a victory for Satan was actually his defeat. God's call triumphed. Years later when the so-called Aucas were reached with the gospel, this became even clearer. It is imperative that church leaders are dependent on the Lord for guidance as they talk with, and prepare, a candidate for ministry.

If agreement of the church is necessary, and if a church refuses to recognize a call even though the person is convinced he or she has received it, what should that person do? William Carey (1761-1834), an early modern missionary, clearly went against the counsel of church leaders when he felt called to do missionary work. But where would missions be today if Carey had heeded the church and ignored his personal sense of calling to India? Is a parallel to be found in the experience of some women who have believed deeply that God has called them to some ministry but have been opposed by church officials who refuse to recognize that call? Should women today who have a sense of calling that is not affirmed by their church follow their sense of calling or follow the church? What about people who feel called to serve in some para-church ministry but who do not have a close enough association with a local church for that church to ratify their sense of call? And does a call from God also imply a responsibility for other people to provide financial support?

These are just some of the questions that revolve around the matter of God's call to ministry and missions. On the one hand, the idea of calling is theologically secure in the context of the biblical premise that God calls his people in a sovereign way to himself. Consequently, he can continue calling those he chooses in successively more specific vocational ways, for example as pastor of an urban church. At the same time, there are practical as well as biblical questions that challenge the idea of a distinct, identifiable call to ministry that is different from that which the laity receive but shared in common by all those who do enter the ministry. Writings on the subject of Christian ministry contain surprisingly little on the nature of the call to ministry. There are some books and booklets intended to help people discern God's call to them, but it has been difficult to find a comprehensive treatment of the idea of a call that covers historical theology, biblical data, actual instances in the lives of ministers and missionaries, and principles for life application.

## Commissioning of the Candidates

Several different terms are used to express the confidence of the church in a candidate. These terms may include *ordination, the laying on of hands,* or some other motion of approval, but all include prayer. Often, there is a combination of actions. This is especially done with specific reference to the practice of ordination. Ordination to ministry as we usually think of it today has no clear precedent in the New Testament. However, it is customary to ask the candidate for ordination a simple question like this: "Do you have a clear call to the ministry?" Any expression of uncertainty at this point could stall, if not block, ordination. If the basis of ordination is a clear call by God, this is an appropriate and necessary question. But how crucial calling may be in any given church or denomination depends in turn on the understanding of what ordination accomplishes. It is useful to note that very different opinions exist regarding the nature and significance of ordination. For some denominations and churches, ordination is simply an acknowledgment that the individual is qualified for a particular ministry. It is a commendation and encouragement to pursue that ministry. In other quarters, however, ordination is believed to change the direction and very nature of the candidate's future life. The Catholic Church teaches that it bestows an indelible character. *Character* in this instance does not simply describe a person's moral qualities. The phrase refers to the idea, put in popular terms, of "once a priest, always a priest." Significant differences, therefore, exist regarding the nature and importance of a call, and these are intertwined with varying concepts of salvation. Most Protestants believe it does not change a life in the sense of the Catholic doctrine.

The term *office* is understood simply to signify a function, service, or duty and may be employed with or without ordination. The word for *office* is not in the New

Testament. *Commendation* is a very loose term and can cover several types of recognition. The *laying on of hands* sounds less official but could have a broad significance. Its use grew as time went on, initially from the privilege of "serving tables" (Acts 6:2) to "the ministry of the word of God" (Acts 6:4), the giving of the Spirit (Acts 8:17), preaching (Acts 13:1–3) and the transfer of gift (1 Tim. 4:14; 2 Tim. 1:6, 7). In short, ordination is a term that gathered more significance as time went on.

How early in life can one expect a person to become conscious of a calling? One might ask how early one should become baptized (if not as an infant). How early should a child be admitted to church membership? The answers depend on the church and the parents, perhaps on the denomination. But being called is unlike these, in that it is the work of the Holy Spirit in relationship to the individual. The answers, of course, will vary wildly and have to be offered differently for each individual. Personally I would urge each Christian family to encourage their children to seek God first, their abilities and interests second, and the possibility of a call third, but always considered.

# 6

# Case Study: A Sending Church

### By Thomas Keppeler

*Thomas Keppeler served in cross-cultural ministry for eighteen years in Europe and now serves as pastor in the mission-serve hub at Elmbrook Church. He holds a PhD from Trinity Evangelical Divinity School and has taught and traveled internationally.*

## Calling and Personal History

I recall as a young teen being fascinated by the film *Jeremiah Johnson* about a nonconformist mountain man who rejected all convention of normal society. I thought what he did was cool, because it bucked convention and he was able to live not only an adventurous life but also one that was surely marked as different. As a young grade-school boy, I wondered if my life path would be like that of my father and grandfather and I would end up in the family business. I recall one Sunday afternoon in the mid 1960s when my grandfather visited our home. He had just given me several old coins for my growing coin collection. (He was an avid coin collector in his retirement.) As I sat on the living room carpet, admiring my Indian-head pennies, my thoughts went like this: *Someday, I'm going to go to high school. Then I will go to college like my dad. Then I will go to work for my dad's company, which he took over from my grandpa. Then I am going to retire and collect coins. Then I'm going to die. I don't want to do that. I want to do something different. I want to be different.* This attitude of nonconformity and wanting to be different, for better or for worse, began to mark my life and experience as a Christian.

In 1979, I was halfway through my senior year of college on a large, secular campus. I heard about a student missionary conference that was going to take place in Urbana, Illinois. It sounded intriguing and I decided to attend. The last evening, Billy Graham preached, and at the conclusion of his message, he issued this challenge: "If you are willing to go anywhere, to do anything, for the sake of the gospel, please stand." I, along with thousands of other college students, stood on my feet. This seemed like such a natural thing to do if I was going to take my Christian faith, and the claims of Christ, seriously. At the time, I did not necessarily understand this to be my call to global missions, but I did know that there was some connection to God's heart for the world and the fact that I rose to my feet in response to Graham's invitation. I do know that I wanted my life to be fully invested into whatever a commitment to Christ and his gospel had in store for me.

Several months later, while still a student on campus, I had a conversation with a campus staff worker of a large para-church ministry that was very active in reaching students on campus. The past two years, I had been very involved with this ministry as a student leader and had grown a lot in my faith and ability to evangelize and disciple. This conversation was "the talk" (given to most student leaders) where he essentially challenged me to consider becoming a full-time staff worker with this same organization because, in his words, this would be truly one of the best ways to invest my life for eternal things. Though I had spent almost five years earning an engineering degree, there was no conversation given to how pursuing engineering as a vocational direction might also be a way to invest my life. In both tone and content, it was clear that full-time Christian work, especially with this particular organization, was a more worthy eternal pursuit. I knew I was interested in vocational ministry, and in particular, this whole area which people referred to as global missions, even though I had little understanding of what that meant. I declined—with the perspective that I wanted to give engineering a try and that if God ever called me to pursue vocational ministry, and especially this thing called global missions, he would make that clear. I didn't want to succumb to the pressure (or the logic) of my campus staff worker.

Immediately out of college, I worked for almost two years in my field of engineering and experienced little satisfaction or internal sense of significance in what I was doing. It didn't help that at that time, the industry was in severe decline and there was not much work to do. At the same time, I enjoyed greatly pouring myself into the youth at my church as a volunteer, and I still had the inklings of pursuing global mission, though I knew very little of what that meant. I also concluded (perhaps prematurely?) that I would continue to experience great frustration and dissatisfaction, and that my soul would shrink if I remained in my current field, with the current company. Under the godly guidance and leadership of an elder from our church, I quit my job and moved back to the Midwest to enroll in graduate school to learn more about God's heart for the world, global mission, and my possible role in that.

The subsequent years have been full and have included finishing a master's degree, eighteen years of cross-cultural missionary service in Europe, and eventually a doctoral degree. For the past nine years, I served on staff at a large, Midwestern church overseeing global mission in a rapidly changing world and an ever-evolving and dynamic mission paradigm. Looking back just on my own personal history, I draw several observations.

An individual's personality, natural abilities, interests, and spiritual gifts all play a role in understanding and discerning calling.

Though I resisted the pressure placed on me to go on staff with the campus organization, I bought into the sacred/secular dichotomy of work and ministry and viewed ministry as the ultimate expression of Christian service and commitment.

I had little or no theology of vocation as a student or young adult. That coupled with my negative experience in my first job in the engineering field were, in part, determining factors pointing me toward pursuing vocational missionary work.

Were these the seeds of something—perhaps a call? Was it a commitment to global missions? I do believe that a commitment to the mission of God was planted in my life as I responded to Graham's challenge at Urbana '79.

# The Transition from Calling to Sending

God's call is immensely greater than just the call to ministry. We may think of a call to ministry as being the highest calling a human being can experience. That opinion is true in some regards but must not be considered apart from the calling that God gives to all believers. Anything that we may consider to be a *special* call takes its meaning and shape from the high calling of God in Christ Jesus. Likewise, a felt calling must not be disassociated from the obligation (and I use that term deliberately) to acknowledge Jesus Christ as Lord of our lives. That is not to say that we make Jesus Lord. Ideally, there should be no interval between our receiving Christ as Savior and our acknowledging him as Lord. We need to accept him as Savior precisely because we have rejected him as Lord, which is the essence of sin, of which we are all guilty. Although in practice we may proceed in the enjoyment of salvation without understanding the implications of Jesus' Lordship, this is not biblically or theologically correct. We may quote, "All have sinned and fall short of the glory of God," realizing that we have indeed sinned, but without realizing what constitutes the core of that sin, which is addressed by the words "come short of the glory of God."

Ideally, commitment to Christ should therefore involve repentance for sin and acknowledgment of the Lordship of Jesus Christ (without pausing here to discuss the sequence of the relevant steps in the *ordo salutis,* the order of salvation). All is within the call of God. No call to ministry—whatever terminology we may use— takes place in isolation from God's call to salvation and obedience. How can one hear a trumpet call to ministry (i.e., unmistakable) unless we are already marching in step to the music?

To express it in a different way, it is not biblically appropriate that we should enjoy the benefits of salvation but delay the decision to obey the will of God in our lives. Obedience should flow out of faith ("Trust and obey," as the old hymn put it). Given the reality of human sinfulness, this obedience *is* often delayed. Therefore, we need such exhortations as Romans 12:1, 2. Our heart's desire should not first be to listen for a call but to be close to the Lord. Then he can lead us in whatever ways he chooses.

We turn now to Walt's analysis of the Old Testament and New Testament and the question of calling. Walt's thoughtful and probing analysis of both Old Testament and New Testament patterns, examples, and narratives that relate to calling suggest a more organic link to the idea that God sends his people into the world. Therefore, I suggest that calling ultimately needs to be understood in light of God's people being a *missional* people (i.e., privileged to participate in the mission of God) and in light of being a *sent* people. Sentness is a newer concept understood in terms of our identity and place in the world. In an earlier chapter, Walt points out that in Scripture, the act of God sending people into various kinds of service appears more frequently than his calling.

The words in New Testament Greek for *appoint, designate* and *apostles* place new emphasis on sending, rather than on just calling. Jesus' appointing the seventy-two in Luke 10, as well as in Mark 3:15, places the emphasis on "sending" and not on calling. The same emphasis on sending can be said of Moses and the command by God to go to Pharaoh and on Isaiah in his prophetic ministry to the people of God (Isa. 6). Sending language is prominent in Joseph's words to his brothers in Genesis 45 as he looks back on all that happened in the providential. "God sent me here to preserve life." God sends Jonah twice (even though at first he disobeys) to Nineveh to proclaim God's message. Jeremiah uses the language of God's sending more than any other prophet, and that sending usually had a great cost in terms of hardship and suffering. Jesus' words to his disciples in John 20:21 remind us that Jesus' sending of his followers is modeled on the Father sending His son into the world. "As the Father has sent me, so I am sending you."

John 3:16-17, one of the most well-known verses used often in evangelistic presentations, is a powerful sending text. "For God so loved the world that he gave His one and only Son, that whoever believes in him shall not perish but have eternal life. For God did not send his Son into the world to condemn the world, but to save the world through him."

Thus, we conclude that all followers of Christ are participants in the mission of God in this world. Closely related to this is that God sends his followers into the world. As we return to our desire to understand the meaning and practical outworking of calling in the life of a believer, we need to understand calling in the broader context of the two aforementioned realities. In other words, all Christians are participants in God's mission to the world, and all are sent into this world, sending being understood as related both to place and identity.

# Mission, Sending, Calling: A Case Study

I have suggested that mission, sending, and calling are related concepts. They are connected not only at a theological level but also at a practical level, as seen through how churches live out their understanding and engagement in God's mission to the world today. I would like to share a few things from my own experience as a pastor of mission in the church as a case study of how we are wrestling with some of these issues at a practical level.

## Background

For over four decades, Elmbrook Church has had an active engagement in both global and local mission. Much of our current missional DNA was influenced greatly by former senior pastor, Stuart Briscoe, who for thirty years not only ministered in the pulpit but also actively traveled and taught internationally during his tenure. He brought back stories and examples of God at work around the world. These stories were often woven into the sermons and teaching Sunday after Sunday. He would often quip in informal conversations that "mission begins between your own two feet."

During the 1970s as Elmbrook experienced significant numerical growth, the size of its mission budget grew and the church began financially supporting missionaries (many who were not from Elmbrook) through traditional mission agencies. As both the church and the mission budget continued to grow into the 1980s, the church began to raise up and send out missionaries from within the congregation. These worked primarily through many of the same mission agencies, but support became limited to those coming from within Elmbrook. This practice continued through the decade of the nineties, and at one time, the church had over 115 financially supported missionaries on its roster.

Beginning around 2000, while continuing its support and sending of career missionaries, the church began to build international partnerships *directly* with churches and ministries in other parts of the world. This included relationships and initiatives in places like Congo, Kenya, Sudan, India, and Indonesia. This kind of engagement arose out of an increasing awareness that our world was changing and that the paradigms of missional engagement in our world was quickly changing as well. The center of gravity of Christianity was no longer in the Western world, and the church of the "global south" was on the move. Looking back on our own history, our engagement as a church in mission fit (albeit in an overlapping way) to a significant degree into three broad approaches. We have supported missions (and missionaries) through agencies, we raise up and send our own home-grown missionaries, but also through agencies, and we build partnerships either with agencies or national churches and organizations around common goals and vision.

Throughout these three paradigms and over the decades, congregation-wide involvement in mission was understood and expressed through financial giving to the mission budget as well as through prayer for our missionaries and global (and eventually local) partners. Involvement beyond that also included opportunities for interested church members to participate in short-term mission trips as well as for a small number to engage in various ways on mission and missionary care-related committees and team. To a significant extent, these engagements continue up to the present.

So what does the future look like? How can we as a church build on and learn from our past while at the same time live out more fully—church-wide—what it means for every Christ follower to understand and participate in the mission of God, understand and live out their sentness, and in that discern their calling? This next section will attempt to lay out some of the practical things we are trying to do.

## Giving People a Picture

The definition of *evangelization* from the Lausanne Covenant has been a very helpful framework for capturing the essence of what it means to engage in the mission of God: the whole church taking the whole gospel to the whole world. In the past year, the area that I oversee—the mission-serve hub—has recast our vision of what we are to be about against this framework, but also in terms of the metaphor of a gardener.

Metaphorically speaking, we talk about "getting dirt under our fingernails," which is a picture that evokes messiness, involvement, and engagement. As a team and hub within the church, we have consequently defined our corporate pastoral task as

> Helping people discern the garden that God is sending them to **cultivate and grow,** whether close to home or on the other side of the world. We pray for, care for, and resource people to serve God in his desire to see individuals and their communities flourish in Christ. This work is messy, but the harvest we hope for means we will get dirt under our fingernails.

Implicit in the metaphor language cited above are

1. the important biblical and missiological concepts of God sending his people
2. that missional engagement is both local and global
3. that it is God's work
4. that it is about seeing people experience the peace and reconciliation that only come through Christ
5. the work does not depend on us but on God.

Success is understood as everyone (a daunting task indeed) at Elmbrook: actively participating in the flourishing of people and communities, whether close to home or on the other side of the world. What does a flourishing person look like? This is a person who lives and loves like Jesus. It is someone who is connected in deepening relationships and participates in the broader body of Christ. A flourishing person is one who uses his or her gifts to serve others at home, work, or wherever they are. It is someone who responds to the love of Christ with generosity and seeks to help others also flourish in Christ. What does a flourishing community look like? A community that is flourishing has families, businesses, schools, arts, entertainment, and organizations that reflect the changes stimulated by flourishing individuals.

We are only at the beginning of trying to live out of and communicate through this metaphor as a mission team, but early signs indicate it is a helpful picture for people to begin to tilt heads and consider that perhaps God has a garden that he is sending them to cultivate.

# The Discipleship Process: Students and Adults

Our adult and student hubs are two important areas of the church where sending is an important concept at the level of the discipleship curriculum.

Our student ministry team has written and piloted an excellent curriculum-conference tandem designed for high school students. Using an intensive, four-day conference format called the GO Conference, students are led through a discipleship curriculum structured around four major themes:

1. GO Big—students are introduced to the grand narrative, or big story of the Bible.

2. GO Deep—students learn how the gospel story begins—with Creation—as well as what it means to have a gospel identity living as family, servants, learners, and sent ones.
3. GO In—focuses on what it means to be a neighbor as you enter the journey of someone else's life.
4. GO Together—emphasizes that we are not sent alone and that our identity as sent ones is living and doing life together.

Though early in its development, the GO Conference and the corresponding curriculum make an excellent application of trying to engage the young generation in the mission of God, to root that engagement in our identity as a sent people while embracing a holistic vision of mission. The whole process and curriculum are built on an understanding of identity rooted in sentness.

The discipleship process used in the adult ministries identifies a number of discernible steps from new believers to unleashing people to participate fully in the mission of God. At each identifiable step, there are intentional, relationship-based opportunities for people to grow in their walk with God, including new believers ("Get in"), faith foundations ("Get grounded"), opportunities for care and support groups ("Get healthy"), and ongoing growth opportunities through small groups ("Grow stronger.").

The last phase in our adult discipleship process is currently being developed and entails equipping people for gospel-centered leadership and impact in the world. We are calling this missional discipleship component

"Unleashed." Though early in its developmental stages, Unleashed is a movement equipping and empowering people for gospel-centered leadership in the world that has three major units.

We discern: As a result of Unleashed, participants will *discern* the call of God in their lives and determine the context in which to live out that *calling*.

We develop: As a result of Unleashed, participants will *develop* a biblical framework to more fully integrate their sense of *calling* and vocation in the mission of God as it relates to their family, workplace, community, and broader world.

We deploy: As a result of Unleashed, participants will be *deployed* with a concrete plan and *calling* to bless their families, influence their communities, and work for the flourishing of their city and the building of God's kingdom.

At the time of this writing, the Unleashed curriculum is still being developed and piloted.

# 7

# Where Does This Leave Us?

As wonderful as the commission narratives of the Old Testament and New Testament are, they should not lead us to assume that in this age of the Spirit and the church we should expect that God's nudging of us through our inner spirit is automatic. We need the accompanying affirmation of the church or, at times, that of a responsible para-church organization. This was illustrated in the previous chapter by Tom Keppeler.

We must never forget that the Bible is not a smorgasbord from which we choose what we want or what we think is nutritious. The Bible is intended to help us to know God and to follow his ways. Moses prayed to God, "If you are pleased with me, teach me your ways so I may know you and continue to find favor with you" (Ex. 33:13). Rather than searching the Bible for clues as to what God wants us to do and whether he has called and sent us, we should read the Bible—including the Old Testament and New Testament narratives—in order to know the way in which God acts in various circumstances so that we can know him better. To do this will not only be of immense help in our praying and in our obeying, but also it will help us walk in a close, intimate fellowship with our Lord. The old saying "A text without its context is a pretext" applies also to passages we search for help on calling.

This leaves us with the great reality that our God is a calling and sending God. He longs to draw us to himself in salvation and in a close, holy life. This is true whether we serve him in the workplace or in some special ministry. It would perhaps be better sometimes to speak of his appointment to special ministries in terms other than calling. The mystery of the word *calling* begins to clear up when we face its ambiguity. It has several meanings and applications in Scripture, and we have tended to use it in contexts and for purposes beyond those in Scripture. In this book, we have also put slightly more emphasis on calling than on sending, a more frequent and significant term in Scripture with regard to the process of entering specialized ministries. Readers should realize that calling is incomplete without sending. When we grasp this, we are on the way to peace of mind and effective ministry.

God has revealed his will for the world: he wants all to hear and no one to perish. Christians who devote themselves to this end are therefore in the will of God. People cannot be saved without hearing the gospel. This requires Christians to take the gospel to those who have not heard it with sufficient clarity to understand and believe. God wants the nations to acknowledge his name and give him glory. Christians therefore must creatively find ways to make God known in truth. This may require new ways of viewing the world. It may demand that you review freshly some materials you studied previously.

God desires the church to grow and be strong. He has provided gifted people to facilitate this, and these people should go where they can best accomplish this task. The call of God has already been issued in the Great Commission. Every believer should proceed to obey this call, trusting God daily to overrule any wrong or unwise decisions. The commission is not a means to hold you in its grip but a means to move you closer and closer to God's view.

God only rarely provides supernatural revelation for individual guidance. Therefore, the Christian believer normally should take steps to go where she or he is most needed in the world, without depending on signs or on subjective impulse. God wants his people to desire to be servant-leaders (1 Tim. 3:1). Christians therefore should offer themselves voluntarily in this direction. It might be that one can find opportunities never thought of to be pressed into service.

The best signs of qualifications for calling are evidence of spiritual maturity and faithfulness in service already accomplished. We can trust God as our Father to assume responsibility for us beyond provision for our normal needs. This can mean rare experiences of seeking him to help us deal with unusual circumstances. It may mean opportunities to seek his direct guidance where others do not seem to need it.

Pray for God's guidance. The emphasis here is not simple. It may require days, perhaps weeks, alone, reading and applying Scripture. It may require extended review of previously held opinions that now need changing. Fasting is not popular today. If it is not a normal procedure, it may be a new way for you to seek God's will. It may require or even demand a difficult process for you to follow.

Allow the Holy Spirit to lead. In conjunction with the items above, this may call for extended and repeated times in God's presence. It may require seeking God to be sure that previously held views on major topics no longer control our thinking. Seek the wisdom of others. This can be tricky. It may mean that we should reject the opinion, and perhaps the influence, of someone who has been meaningful to us. It may mean that we have to form a new group of friends. Seek external confirmation from friends, local church, sending agency, and those who receive ministry from us, based on gifts, preparation, relationships, and support.

Seek internal inspiration (God's peace, joy, vision for opportunities). There is more in Scripture about calling and sending for all believers than there is about individual calling; therefore, actively serve God together with others. In this category are closely held values. Don't be discouraged by negative views about missions that others may have. It takes a while for some new ideas to be accepted. Be sure that your personal views reach out to others. Realize that nothing replaces character. You know yourself better than do others. Little opportunities to help others are important. Keep close watch on your expenditure of time. Hours wasted in movies, TV, and similar opportunities quickly add up.

For some, involvement in ministry before involvement in education may be more important than it may appear. Take opportunities to seek the advice and encouragement of spiritual leaders. Choose people to follow in life tentatively before making commitments that are hard to break. Seek ministry mentors who will equip you and give you feedback.

Don't enter ministry out of your own personal emotional needs. This is an especially important area for you to control. Be sure that you know step by step what God wants before making decisions; begin to move in the direction you believe God is leading you. Compare the inner call with outwardly visible indicators. God's will for right now is to pray, witness, learn, and obey his will revealed in all the Scriptures. It is to move purposefully toward whatever next step will enable you to obey the Great Commission more fully.

Calling is not separate from the total work of God in our lives. The concern of each of us should be to keep close to God, meet with him regularly, keep the Word of God in mind and heart, obey him in matters great and small, and consciously seek to serve him in whatever circumstances we may be.

## Practical Suggestions

In order to make this practical, I interviewed a number of people involved in ministry as to how they were called to ministry and others in secular work regarding what called them into their field. Here are some actual responses to a survey I conducted among missionaries, pastors, teachers, IVCF staff, and others as to what brought about their sense of God's call to Christian or secular work. These are, or arise from, actual events.

## Scripture and Prayer

Being sensitive to God's Word.
Gradual conviction through Scripture.
The influence of James 1:22-25.
Develop your relationship with God first.
Do not assume too easily or quickly that you know exactly
what God wants.
An objective indication from God while praying.
Hearing an exposition of Genesis 38-40 one month after
conversion.

## Counsel

The input of your church leaders is vital.
Discuss your feeling openly with your spouse, friends, and
others knowledgeable of the opportunities.
Direction from a pastor and from the church.
Seek pastor's advice.
Confirmation by other Christians, but also an objective
indication from God while praying, plus a remarkable
provision of financial help.

## Responding to Need

Sensing the need in a particular country.
Seeing the need everywhere for biblical preaching.

## Experience

One year of personal experience teaching in a mission school.

Through such diverse experiences as living in China for a year and reading Chaim Potok's book *The Chosen*.

By being one of God's chosen people, responding to opportunities of service.

## Leaving Secular Employment

I have not had a subjective experiential call; rather, my growing sense of giftedness and knowledge of needs led me to transition from secular employment to vocational Christian service. The church confirmed this.

For most, if not all, of my business life, I sensed that God was moving me in the direction of full-time ministry.

A combination of a mostly auditory vision impressions from God that I was not to be an engineer all my life, followed by an unexpected, appropriate comment by a friend, plus the teaching of Scripture.

Impediments to furthering a career of some years in law.

## Giftedness

A sense of personal giftedness.

Gradually, mainly through an inner sense of calling, but also through a sense of personal giftedness and perceived needs.

Seeing the response to my speaking at a conference and then gradual awareness of a call.

Inner sense of calling, but call was never defined as I talked with many people.

Seeing the response to my speaking at an Easter dawn service.

## Don't Wait

Be active in ministry before you go to get educated for
ministry.
Begin to move in the direction you believe God is calling you.
As you serve the Lord where you are, be open to new moves.
Don't look for signs; just get going.
Serve.
Make sure you *do* have a call. It will give you encouragement
in the inevitable hard trials to come.

## Examples

I looked at the lives of missionary friends and relatives.
I observed the lives of missionary parents and others.

## Leaving an Overseas Ministry

A missionary who then returned to the United States
with the heartfelt belief that he would be serving God in
medical publishing just as much as when he was on the
mission field.

## Other

I believe a sense of adventure and desire for cross-cultural
experience might have had more to do with my calling
(passion, gift, personality) than anything.

I would never have married someone who did not
also feel called.

Hearing the academic dean say, "If you can be anywhere else doing anything else, then you should leave," and thinking, *I can't.*

The various experiences here, along with others we see in this book, testify to the evidence that God is not confined to any one, or set of, ways. He works with complete freedom to draw people to himself and to assign tasks to them that he chooses to be appropriate.

## The Question of One's Calling

Finally, I would like to offer the following, which is an example of the influence of short-term mission trips. This article, "Chaos and Grace in the Slums of the Earth," by Kent Annan, appeared in *Christianity Today* (September 2013, pp. 26–32). One of the missionaries Annan interviewed in Bangkok, Thailand, was Michelle Kao. While Kao was a premed student, she visited Bangkok with InterVarsity's urban trek mission. This brought about a turning point in her life. Instead of going on to med school, she returned to Bangkok, joining servant partners. A part of Annan's interview with Kao caught my eye. She said,

> I love what I do. But a while ago, I was questioning my calling. I had this idea that once you discovered your calling, you'd feel fulfilled, like you had *made it.* There were parts that still felt difficult and unclear, and even now, I have questions about whether what I do makes a difference.

So I called some friends in the States. I was wondering if they had figured everything out. To my surprise, every one of them felt like I did. It was good to be reminded that only God can ultimately fulfill. I feel like I've found a home in this community.

Her programs are small. She provides seventeen scholarships for high schoolers, trains community leaders, leads a tiny house church, and cares for a couple of dozen children after school. Might she have had greater impact as a doctor? Yet watching Kao work with such joy and fluency, seemingly so clearly in the right place, brings to mind a question about our own vocations: how are my talents and efforts responding to the world's deep needs?

## The Next Steps

It is clear that both calling and sending face a new age. Calling needs to be fully understood and appreciated, and sending is lively with new possibilities. Calling has been overlooked, and sending always stands at the beginning of new usefulness. This book began some years ago and has persisted through various experiences. The helpfulness of the book with regard to calling is to provide biblical perspectives that may have been missed. One can simply reread the opening chapters looking for ways to enter the various circumstances freshly, with expectation of new blessings. Look for ways to appreciate what God has been doing and what he can now do in your life. Think of his strength. Think of his wisdom. Think of ways he has entered the lives of others. Think of how he has led his people to do the right thing to conquer the enemy. Especially think about your relationship with the Lord and how he is working in your life. Above all, see if there are ways to shape your life more accurately to please God. The busyness of sending will be mere activism if it is not based on calling.

As for sending, the possibilities are without limits. The sections on that topic in this book contain multiple suggestions that have worked well so far in the Elmbrook church as Tom has shared. There will no doubt be changes and new directions. Some aspects of it may, in fact, be changed by the time you read this. It will be well to keep the book handy, consult it from time to time, and work out new directions for the group or church where you are. I do not want to force the ideas in this book on you, but to help you keep awake to what is happening. God is calling and sending, and God is moving, this very day.

Calling is God's sovereign work in our lives; it is his responsibility, not ours. It is not an elusive maneuver of God, a puzzle that we must desperately try to solve. It is a work of grace, as is our salvation, so we can trust and rest. We might say that, somewhat like salvation, calling is the intersection of God's story and ours, the overlapping of God's purposes and our intelligent response and the agreement of God's sovereignty and our obedience. To seek an understanding of God's calling is not some cold analytical process but a passionate desire to know God and his ways and to glorify him in our lives.

# Moved by God

| **Called** | **Sent** |
|---|---|
| Invitation | Command |
| Hands laid: ordination | Feet ready: evangelization |
| Love God | Love neighbor |
| Serve God | Wash feet |
| Fear God | Feed others |
| Honor God | Represent God |
| Come and be | Go and do |
| Who we are | What we become |
| Called to come | Sent to go |
| Be holy | Do good works |
| Coming to God | Going from God |

Peter Fleming did not fulfill all of the above list. In his brief life of twenty-seven years, he made great progress, far more than most do. We will not fully know during our human lifetimes how God will "work all things together for good" to fulfill his calling in each of our lives (Rom. 8:28). We do know that "God's gifts and his call are irrevocable" (Rom. 11:29) and that they will bring glory to him and good to us.

May God grant each of us to give our all to the Lord.